Love Knots

Stories of Faith, Family, and Friendships

Strengthen your relationships in forty days

Featured Authors

Ed Chappelle, Amanda Eldridge, Maria T. Henriksen, Karen Jurgens,
Julie Souza Bradley Lilly, Lee Ann Mancini, Sandra Stein, Shanda
Neighbors, Stephanie Pavlantos, Glenda Shouse, Diane Virginia,
Evelyn Mason Wells, Martin Wiles

Edited and Compiled by

Karen Jurgens, Stephanie Pavlantos, Diane Virginia

Authors:

Ed Chappelle, Amanda Eldridge, Maria T. Henriksen, Karen Jurgens, Julie Souza Bradley Lilly, Lee Ann Mancini, Sandra Stein, Shanda Neighbors, Stephanie Pavlantos, Glenda Shouse, Diane Virginia, Evelyn Mason Wells, Martin Wiles

Editors/Compilers:

Karen Jurgens, Senior Editor; Stephanie Pavlantos, Social Media Senior Editor/Director; Diane Virginia, Founder/Administrator/Lead Editor of VineWords Publishing https://www.vinewords.net

Cover and Interior Design Artists:

Victor Marcos, Omar Marcos https://victormarcosart.portfoliobox.net

Squiggles: Diane Virginia

Typesetter:

Samantha Fury http://www.furycoverdesign.com/fury-covers.html

Library of Congress Control Number: 2020910051

Love Knots: Stories of Faith, Family, and Friendships
Devotional: Forty heartfelt devotions knit together into a love knot are designed to bring you peace and comfort. Strengthen your relationships as you journey through stories of faith, family, and friendship.

ISBN (Paperback) 978-1-7351564-0-8 (e-book) 978-1-7351564-1-5

Unless otherwise indicated, Scripture quotations are taken from THE HOLY BIBLE, NEW KING JAMES VERSION. Copyright 1982 by Thomas Nelson, Inc. Used with permission. All rights reserved.

Scripture quotations marked ESV are taken from the *English Standard Version*. Copyright © 2010. Used by permission of Crossway Publishers, London, England. All rights reserved.

Scripture quotations marked NASB are taken from the *New American Standard Bible,* copyright © 1995. Used by permission of The Lockman Foundation, LaHabra, California. All rights reserved.

Vine Words Publishing

P.O. Box 681, Germanton, NC 27019

https://www.vinewords.net

Glorifying the True Vine, Jesus Christ.
Bearing fruit through our connection with Him.
I [Jesus] am the true vine …
He who abides in Me, and I in Him, bears much fruit.
~John 15:1a, 5a NKJV

Love is not just a fuzzy feeling, it's a choice. The authors of **Love Knots: Stories of Faith, Family, and Friendships** *bare their souls to take us on a realistic journey through life's challenges and celebrations through the use of poetry, stories, and Bible truths. This helps the reader learn to love like Jesus and strengthen their relationships with God, family, and friends. I highly recommend* **Love Knots.** *There is something for everyone in this devotional.*

Cherrilynn Ryerson Bisbano

Award-winning Writer, Coach, Editor; Speaker, Women's Speakers; Partner, The Write Coach Team; former Managing Editor, Almost an Author; two-time winner, Flash Fiction Weekly; Contributor, award-winning books; Navy and Air National Guard Servicewoman, earning the John Levitow Military Leadership Award; Author, *Shine Don't Whine*

I am richer in love for reading **Love Knots: Stories of Faith, Family, and Friendships**, *and am confident everyone who reads this book will be richer too. These testimonies have the potential of providing a hope-filled affirmation of love, which is an innate human need. This helps the reader discover Jesus, the source of holy, unconditional love.*

I would like to see groups of people use this book as the impetus to effect change by promoting the love of Christ in their communities.

Pamela Christian

Ordained International Apostle/Evangelist, with an Honorary Doctorate of Divinity, certified in apologetics (Biola); award-winning Author, Speaker, Teacher, and Media Host; Founder of Pamela Christian Ministries

What a beautiful journey of hope! 40 Days wrapped in God's love and peace is exactly where I want to be found.

Pam Farrel

Author of 50+ books, including bestselling *Men Are Like Waffles, Women Are Like Spaghetti*

I can think of no better way to begin each morning than with the acknowledgement of God's love and peace for us, and a reminder of the great potential for His love and peace to shine through us. **Love Knots: Stories of Faith, Family, and Friendships** *brings together the voices of varied experiences to encourage spiritual growth and scripture meditation, while emphasizing the most important relationships of our daily walk. A refreshing collection sure to prepare you for the day ahead.*

David Holcomb

Discipleship Pastor, River Oaks Community Church, Clemmons, North Carolina

Love Knots: Stories of Faith, Family and Friendships, *renders God's modern-day stories through prose and poetry, drawing us closer to Him. From an earthquake in a baseball stadium, to a child's "messterpiece" to a slice of cake,* **Love Knots** *promises to strengthen our relationships in forty days. It delivers, in short devotions, is rich in the telling, and abundant in scripture. You will come away with a deeper walk with our Lord and with others.*

Renee Leonard Kennedy

President, Word Weavers Piedmont Triad, North Carolina

I found **Love Knots: Stories of Faith, Family, and Friendships** to be one of the hidden gems for God's people at such a time as this. It is filled with down-home stories that come to life. It is a delightful read that captures the essence of everyday examples of a loving Lord.

Because **Love Knots** is a compilation, this gives you the freedom to read and pick up at your leisure.

You can feel the Holy Spirit of God in the pages. This is a must-read.

Charles E. Maldon, Jr.

Founder/Administrator, Naked But Not Ashamed--Men's Ministry, Sylvan Vista Baptist Church, Fairmount Heights, Maryland

Love Knots: Stories of Faith, Family, and Friendships is a "spiritual feast" for the Bride of Christ that I highly recommend you add to your reading list.

I pray the Holy Spirit will move through this devotional, allowing God's Kingdom light to pierce through the darkness. I pray more fire, glory, and splendor as you read these stories. May God breathe into you His love, compassion, unity, and power. In Jesus's Name, Amen.

Victor Marcos

Pastor/Missionary to Lima, Peru; Artist, Virginia Beach, Virginia
Jeremiah 31, Isaiah 61, Isaiah 40

Love Knots: Stories of Faith, Family, and Friendships is like a thick, fluffy and warm crocheted blanket into which you can snuggle and be blessed with wisdom, truth, encouragement, and inspiration.

Each author's contributions is varied and unique. Every single person can benefit from something in this collection, but I'm sure every person will benefit from everything in this collection.

I was blessed by reading these heart-warming stories.

Kathy Collard Miller

Author of *God's Intriguing Questions* and *No More Anger: Hope for an Out-of-Control Mom*

In reading the devotions in **Love Knots: Stories of Faith, Family, and Friendships***, I felt as if my Heavenly Father had invited me to sit with Him while He shared with me some of His treasures. The invitation is a continual one. I will be a back often.*

Susan Powell Miller

Christian Counselor and Teacher, The Bridge Counseling Center, Kernersville, North Carolina

The book you are holding consists of inspirational stories sure to transform and reshape your faith. During these stressful and uncertain times, we need access to a book that can equip us to understand our loving God who is ever-near, in good times and in bad.

Love Knots: Stories of Faith, Family, and Friendships *is a book in season. Easing anxiety and offering assurance of God's unending love for all of creation. As you read each powerful compilation, may you realize Christ as your Cornerstone who lovingly holds all things together...even us!*

LaTan Roland Murphy

Award winning Author of *Courageous Women of the Bible* writer, speaker, decorator, lover of people and strong coffee

Imagine a book that could transform your relationships. A book with that kind of influence would be filled with stories of love, scriptures of peace, powerful insights, and faith boosters. **Love Knots: Stories of Faith, Family, and Friendships** *is that book, and to activate its power, all you need to do is read it.*

Linda Evans Shepherd

Bestselling, Award winning Author of *Empowered for Purpose, When You Need to Move a Mountain,* and numerous other books; International Speaker; President, Right to the Heart Ministries; CEO, Advanced Writers and Speakers Association (AWSA); Publisher, Leading Hearts Magazine, and Arise Daily, of AWSA.

In the military, my life and the lives of fellow soldiers depended upon my knowing how to select the right knot needed for any situation and my ability to tie it properly. Knot-tying became second nature, and I found myself tying them instinctively.

An important fact about knots is that knots have the ability to untie themselves over time, so they must be checked and re-tied to ensure their connection is secure.

Love Knots: Stories of Faith, Family, and Friendships *provides readers with an arsenal of over forty ways to connect to God and allow Him to anchor your life.*

With each devotion, you learn to use and depend upon the love knot to ensure your bond with our Creator remains secure.

J.D. Winniger

Follower of God, Writer, Speaker, & Friend

FOREWORD

I heard it while I was praying. Just a whisper within my spirit— *Love Knots*. I continued to pray, but heard that inner nudge again. And then again... Finally, I realized this was not a random thought; it was a message from God. I asked Him to explain. ***Love Knots: Stories of Faith, Family, and Friendships*** is what I heard next. As a writer, I recognized God was communicating a book title.

I researched and discovered the love knot is a crochet stitch, and an alternate name is the "Solomon's knot." This I found fascinating because the main characters in the biblical vignette, Song of Solomon, are "Love" and "Beloved," representative of the Bride of Christ, and the Bridegroom, Jesus Christ. In the vignette, the Bridegroom's allegorical name, "Beloved Solomon," comes from two Hebraic words meaning divine love and peace, and this joyful state is made available to the Bride as she abides in His presence.

There it was—the meaning of the love knot revealed.

As we abide in the presence of our Savior, we should expect His divine love and peace to become available to us. This will affect every relationship, starting with our faith-relationship with Jesus Christ and extending to our relationships with family and friends.

Is the Solomon's knot found in Scripture? Yes. It was an adornment carved into the base of the Temple pillars of the Holy Place and the Holy of Holies and overlaid with pure gold (see 1 Kings 6:18 KJV), and again as a two-row adornment carved into the brazen laver used to purify the priests (see 1 Kings 7:24 KJV). We don't perceive this as being the love knot because of the wording. *Knop*, in the King James, in essence, means love knot.

I believe the significance of the biblical usage of the love knot is a hidden gem, symbolizing the love God has had for us from the beginning of history. Just think—He loves us so much He carved love knot ornamentations in the holiest of places.

Consider the activity that took place in the Holy of Holies and its outer court. Worship and giving oneself to God in total surrender happened there. This was but a shadow of the worship we can experience today.

As New Testament believers with the Spirit of Christ living within us, we are His living temples. Peter describes us as "a chosen generation, a royal priesthood, a holy nation, His own special people" (1 Peter 2:9a NKJV). And this we become, so we may "proclaim the praises of Him who called you out of darkness into His marvelous light" (1 Peter 2:9b NKJV).

Our prayer for you, dear reader, is that as you read these stories, the love knot of God's peace will become as a truth stitched within your heart. We pray Jesus Christ will crochet into your life a love so rich it will take over every thought and every action until you are fully His as He is yours. In every relationship—from your faith journey to your family dynamics, and in every friendship—the Lord has ordained His love knot of peace in the relational bond.

Once I realized this was a book we should prepare, I asked our team of writers to contribute in the three areas, and we enthusiastically took on this task. As our leader team compiled, evaluated, and edited the stories, we found it necessary to have tissues handy. Oh, how we cherished the tears.

In the Bible, the number forty is associated with change, so we made this a forty-day devotional with the hope that as you read these stories, they might serve to refresh you as God works healing into your mind, soul, and spirit.

Press into the common thread running through each devotion and into the love knot where God's love and peace dwells. When you read a writer's story about a painful situation, notice how God shows up every time. Why is this important? God wants to work in your life in a similar way.

What have we tucked inside this devotional? Each author has approached this assignment with his/her unique life-experience, so you will find a variety of stories, but each is unified by the love knot.

In the **Faith** section, we share stories about God's limitless, lavish love, as well as God working His peace in the midst of persecution. We share a life transformed from "messterpiece" to "masterpiece;" a person receiving mercy beyond forgiveness; a person conquering persecution through perservering faith; a foundational truth that rocks the world; and obedience learned while someone watches an individual picking up rocks.

In the **Family** section, we share stories of godly upbringings; a fatherless child who finds a godly mentor; family pets who receive prayer; a marriage bond growing stronger despite a husband receiving a life-altering medical diagnosis; a grieving widow becoming whole again; a vivid, God-ordained dream directing family values; and a little girl, aged four-and-a-half, dancing for Jesus.

In the **Friendships** section, we share stories of friends becoming spiritual mothers; a homeless man who finds direction; a prayer for the prodigal; unusual, God-ordained friendships where the Lord alone causes a unity; a friendship birthed out of an act of obedience; military men/women worthy of honor; and daisy petals affirming God's love.

Are you ready to look for the love knot? Well then, snuggle into your favorite chair, shut out the distractions of life, find some tissues, and turn the page. Your personal discovery of Jesus's love knot He wants to crochet into your life is about to begin.

Shalom,

ACKNOWLEDGEMENTS

There are many people we are grateful to who made *Love Knots: Stories of Faith, Family, and Friendships* a reality. I wish to acknowledge them on our team's behalf.

To the reader, thank you for purchasing and sharing this book. I hope you will perceive this as our way of giving you a smile, and a heartfelt tear, but most of all—the love knot of God's peace. The Lord is ever present, working amongst us in every season of life, and we pray you will benefit from the heartfelt testimonies tucked within these pages.

To our book endorsers, we greatly appreciate you for taking the time to review this devotional and for putting your stamp of approval on it. Your kind words are a blessing, and we pray God will bless you abundantly for sanctioning our endeavour.

To our contributing authors, thank you for your commitment to draw readers to the Lord Jesus Christ, and for being vulnerable enough to share the stories God Himself placed within your hearts—for these are your own personal love knot experiences. Thank you, authors, for being men and women of great character. Because of your hard work, team spirit, enthusiasm, and grace, we have accomplished our goal.

Thanks goes to every leader, teacher, and servant of the Asheville Christian Writer's Conference (ACWC), Blue Ridge Christian Writer's Conference (BRCWC), and other conferences we have participated in. Thank you for teaching us the craft of writing. We've done some learnin' from your teams, and this is our attempt, as you've taught us, to follow the Christian writer's battle cry. Without you, we could not have done this, and we are grateful.

Thank you, Eddie Jones, for mentoring me when I brought this devotional idea to you at the 2019 ACWC. You advised me wisely, and I reflected on your counsel often as our team put this book together. You instilled in me the confidence and courage to make sound decisions, and the knowledge this could be a success, if done correctly. Thank you for caring, and for imparting wisdom from your many years in the writing ministry.

Thank you, Karen Jurgens, for being the Senior Editor of this project. You reviewed every story multiple times with a keen attention to detail, and with the *Chicago Manual of Style* in hand. You worked evenings, often into the wee hours of the morning, as we exchanged documents to perfect this work. I cherish these memories not only because we made progress, but because we prayed as we did so. This speaks well of your character, and of the Spirit who leads you.

Thank you, Stephanie Pavlantos, for taking on the task of Social Media Senior Editor/Director. Thank you for your compiling and editing the media work, for creating content for our social media pages, for tweeting, securing interviews, and for performing other promotional actions. I admire your energy, scholarly excellence, perseverance, moderation, and your confidence to try new things. But most of all, I value our friendship because you are a Spirit-led woman.

Thank you, my sisters Karen and Stephanie, for your friendship, wise counsel, encouragement, patience, compassion, godliness, and prayers. You were wise enough to meet with me virtually during pivotal moments so we could seek the Lord's direction. I knew with the first such meeting, we would achieve our goal. Ladies, you are to me, as Aaron and Hur were to Moses, and I am most grateful.

To my dear spiritual sister Glenda Shouse, over the twenty-plus years of our sisterhood, you have been a picture of selfless love and a powerhouse of prayer, and you have provided the most encouragement and godly advice of any person save my husband. Thank you for sending scriptures, encouraging notes, and for checking on the progress of all my writing projects—including this one. Thank you for being attuned to Father God's heart, and for knowing intuitively when and how to pray.

To Julie Lilly, thank you for noticing needs and pitching in with the heart of a servant, never expecting any accolades, and for praying on-the-spot with our writers. You, dear sister, exude humility.

To our writers, again I express thanks, but this on a personal level. Every story—EVERY SINGLE ONE—I needed for my own personal growth. Thank you for answering God's call to write.

To Pastor Victor Marcos and son Omar Marcos, thank you for being champion artists by creating the cover design and interior artwork. But also, my dear brothers, thank you for your godly character.

Thank you brother Victor, for sending scriptures, messages, and prophetic words, and for praying with me during every phone consultation we had regarding *Love Knots*. You have the heart of a servant-pastor, and I thank you not only for your prayer coverage during this project, but also for your prayer coverage for our family spanning the eleven-plus years my husband and I have known you.

To Samantha Fury, our typesetter, thank you for your advice, attention to detail, professional skill, and availability. Your skills are most appreciated. You scanned the manuscript several times, and your quick turn-around times were a blessing. Thank you also for being a kind, dedicated, servant of Christ.

To my son, daughter, and son-of-the-heart, Danielle, Matthew, and Eric, thank you for believing in this writing journey, for listening to the stories throughout the years, and for celebrating every milestone. Thank you for giving constructive criticism, and for making sure the cowdoggies and Izzy listened too. Your support has meant a lot to this mommy heart.

To my husband Phil, thank you for your unwavering support. You stayed seated while I retyped a story, saying, "just a sec," so I could read it to you—*again*. You knew full well the "sec" would be much longer than a real second, but you stayed seated because you cared. I do believe I re-read stories to you enough times that you've memorized most of them. Thank you also for your 3 a.m. deliveries of chocolates, crackers 'n cheese, and beverages, so I could keep writing and editing. Thank you for never complaining about peanut butter for dinner—or no dinner—and for periodically putting in a load of laundry so I could stay on task. Thank you for keeping an eye on the weather on the evening we had tornado warnings near our area. When you alerted me of impending danger and I answered "sure," you knew since I was in the "writer's zone," I wasn't really listening. You remained alert, ready to whisk me to the basement, knowing if you told me again about the tornadic weather, you'd get the same vague answer. Writers understand "the zone," and so did you.

To Jesus Christ, who gave me the "love knots" nudge when my schedule was slammed-packed, thank You. Because You have worked within our team of writers, artists, editors, typesetter, and compilers, Your love knot of peace, we were able to bring forth this devotional. You deserve every accolade—we are only Your servants. Our Beloved Savior Jesus Christ, we anticipate Your next divine nudge.

Shalom,

Diane Virginia

To our Lord

and Savior

Jesus Christ,

You are our inspiration, and the reason we share our stories.

May these testimonies of the love knot of divine peace You

worked

within our

hearts

become a

healing

balm to

readers

across

the globe.

TABLE OF CONTENTS

Faith

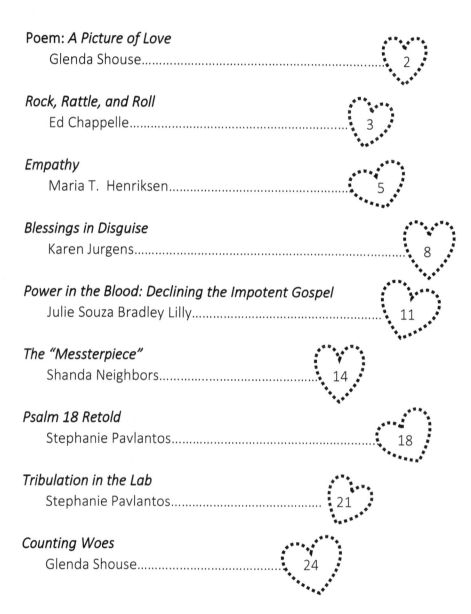

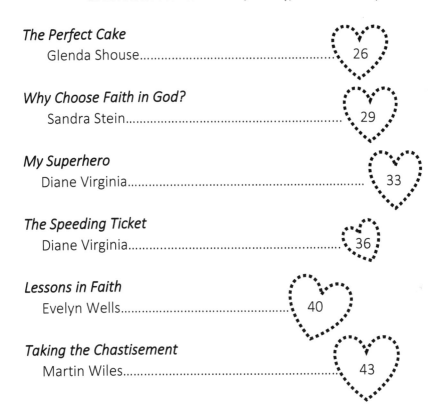
Family

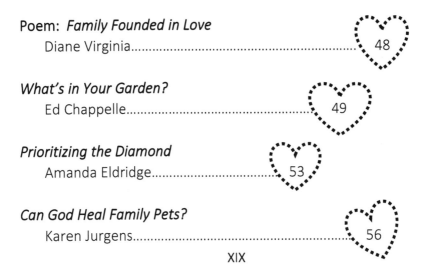

Friendships

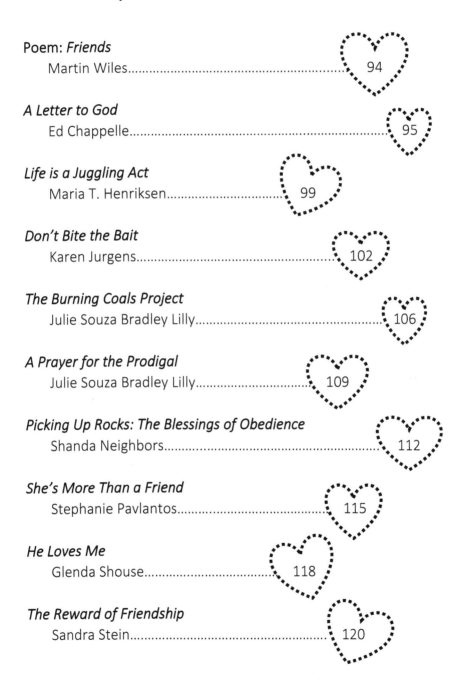

Faith

A Picture of Love

Glenda Shouse

How do you draw a picture of Love?

How do you paint afresh the agony of the Cross?

With gentle strokes of tenderness

as His grace beckons us closer.

There to wash pure white the canvas of our soul.

Then on that clean canvas He paints

layer by layer the beauty of His love.

The picture of love is our Savior's face as He reveals it to us.

How do you see the Master's face?

I'll show you the way.

Look up at the sky and count the stars,

then out over the wide countryside.

Look down from majestic mountain top.

Look into the face of a newborn child.

There you will see the Master's face.

Rock, Rattle, and Roll

Ed Chappelle

For no one can lay a foundation other than that which is laid, which is Jesus Christ.

~1 Corinthians 3:11 ESV

It was another hot and windless day on October 17, 1989. There was a sense of electricity in the air as anticipation built. This game would be number three of the World Series' play-offs. The contest was scheduled to begin at 5:35 p.m. The San Francisco Giants and the Oakland A's were going through the pre-game ceremonies at Candlestick Park in San Francisco, California.

However, things were about to change as the clock moved closer to 5:04 p.m. At that precise moment, the stadium started to rock, rattle, and roll as an earthquake with a magnitude of 6.9 on the Richter scale and a maximum shock intensity hit the city. This earthquake was responsible for sixty-three deaths and 3,757 injuries as the foundations of the surrounding buildings crumbled.

Friends, at any particular moment our lives can rock, rattle, or roll. With one phone call, one trip to the shopping mall, or even a night out at a movie theater, our lives can be shattered with bad news. We are not guaranteed another day of life. In fact, we are not promised even one more moment.

With such an unstable world, we must discover the Cornerstone, the Tested Stone, the One who is the Sure Foundation. Jesus is the One in whom we must ground ourselves in order to survive these uncertain times and sudden calamities. Only He can overcome the tribulations of this world and give us peace amidst the uncertainty.

Isaiah 28:16 ESV assures us, "Therefore thus says the Lord GOD: 'Behold, I am the one who has laid as a foundation in Zion, a stone, a tested stone, a precious cornerstone, of a sure foundation:' Whoever believes will not be in haste." In John we read, "In the world, you will have tribulation. But take heart; I have overcome the world" (John 16:33 ESV).

The good news is we can survive the uncertainty by placing our faith in our Lord and Savior Jesus Christ. By this simple act, we can experience the perfect peace that comes only through abiding in Him.

With such an unstable world, we must discover the Cornerstone, the Tested Stone, the One who is the Sure Foundation.

~Ed Chappelle

I pray each of us will build our lives on Jesus Christ, for upon this Cornerstone, we will remain stable. He is the One who brings to our spirits perfect peace even though the world remains inundated with tribulations of all kinds—physical, emotional, and spiritual.

As we fix our eyes on Jesus Christ alone, He enables us to remain unmovable, unshaken, and inoculated from the rock, rattle, and roll of this unstable world.

Share how Jesus Christ, the Cornerstone, steadies your faith.

Lord Jesus, You are the Cornerstone of my faith. Thank You for being the One who lifts me above the calamity of this world. With You in my heart, I can remain at peace.

Amen.

4

Empathy

Maria T. Henriksen

Do not be afraid nor dismayed because of this great multitude, for the battle is not yours, but God's.

~2 Chronicles 20:15b NKJV

God breathed air into my lungs as I prayed....

I was walking along the beach, struggling with the uncertainty of my children's futures. Having boy/girl twins in their senior year in high school is stressful during normal circumstances.

Then suddenly, everything changed.

Fear of contracting the COVID19 virus turned my family's lives upside-down. Governing bodies mandated us to shelter in place. We were permitted to go out for necessities only, and then we wore masks and practiced "social distancing," staying six feet away from others.

Until the panic caused by the pandemic passed, lockdown would be the "new normal."

I felt like my children's senior year had been snatched from them. They expressed that learning online was a challenge. Equally disheartening was the process of committing to colleges. Since the duration of the lockdown was uncertain, I did not know if they would be permitted to attend a university or college.

Never before in modern history had there been so much uncertainty, as this pandemic spread around the world.

This was not how I had envisioned my children's futures. My heart broke. I was overcome with sadness as I watched them express feelings of shock, frustration, being cheated, missing their friends and teachers. My children had been robbed of their glory days.

The battle belongs to Jesus Christ, not to us.

~Maria T. Henriksen

Then God spoke to me.

As the waves crashed on the sandy beach, the Lord reminded me this situation was temporary, but He was eternal. I need only put my faith in Him. God was in control, and He was faithful.

I found comfort in reciting 2 Chronicles 20:15 NKJV, "'Do not be afraid nor dismayed because of this great multitude, for the battle is not yours, but God's.'"

The fact remained, we were in a global war against the Coronavirus. But I could encourage my family to draw from the waters of hope by remembering God had a plan for each of us. As we sought His will, He would lead us through to victory.

I journaled my thoughts as a poem:

Empathy.

Will it be the death of me?

My mind is swirling. My heart is aching.

My eyes are tearing. My soul is searching.

I cry. I pray. I seek.

I wonder why....

Sinking deeper and deeper, I see the signs.

I find my resolve. I start to climb.

O how God is my Keeper.

Empathy.

O God, I must be strong for Thee.

I choose to put my trust in Thee.

With the guidance of the Holy Spirit, I realised could help my children determine their destinies, knowing God would reveal His plan over time. I needed to walk in faith, and model my trust in Him, being certain God would breathe life into each of us.

God is like the wave, washing us with love no matter the difficulty we may face.

Friend, no matter what you are facing, the battle belongs to Jesus Christ, not to you. Trust Him to guide you through uncertain times, just as He guided my family.

Put your trust in the One who is faithful. He has a plan for you, His love is eternal, and He will see you through.

How do you maintain faith during uncertain times?

Father God, give me the strength, courage, and wisdom to set a good example for my children by maintaining strong faith in You no matter the circumstances. When I face uncertain times, remind me that You alone are my Rock and Fortress. Wash over me with waves of love.

In Jesus Christ's Name, Amen.

Blessings in Disguise

Karen Jurgens

For it is by grace you have been saved, through faith—and this is not from yourselves, it is the gift of God—not by works, so that no one can boast.

~Ephesians 2:8-9 NKJV

What an auspicious day it was when I learned about the nutritious benefits of raw foods. Or was it?

An entire aisle of raw nutrition at an organic grocery popped into view shortly thereafter, and the granola bars almost leapt off the shelf and into my hands.

Although I had discovered these treats were tough to bite into, I indulged for several delicious days. That is—until the fourth day. I bit into a bar that must have sat on a grocery shelf too long. This stubborn bar fought my desire to consume it, and suddenly my tooth bent backward.

That's how I wound up in the endodontist's chair the next morning for a root canal procedure. A tiny but very old infection had been hiding inside an original root canal, and it had remained undetected. Had it continued any longer, it would have caused terrible pain, and the cost to replace the diseased tooth would have been astronomical.

By catching this situation early, it was a blessing in disguise!

This experience got me thinking. Like hidden infections, sin can hide in our spirits, undetected. Although as Christians, we are all sinners saved by grace, we are still capable of harboring "pet sins" in our lives.

James addresses this issue, "Therefore, to him who knows to do good and does not do it, to him it is sin" (James 4:17 NKJV).

King David understood how important it was to ask God to search his heart for hidden sin. He penned, "Search me, O God, and know my heart; try me, and know my anxieties; and see if there is any wicked way in me and lead me in the way everlasting" (Psalm 139:23-24 NKJV).

How can we know if we are harboring undetected sin in our lives? We begin by humbling ourselves in prayer, and we ask the Holy Spirit to search our hearts.

When we understand that pride shrouds sin in darkness, but humility exposes it to the light, this process becomes easier to acquiesce to.

Like hidden infections, sin can hide in our spirits, undetected.

~Karen Jurgens

Left undetected, sin festers and grows, making our spirits sick. But as soon as we recognize it is there, we can go to the One who made a way for us to receive forgiveness, and we can make a fresh start.

John explains this clearly, "If we confess our sins, He is faithful and just to forgive us our sins and to cleanse of all unrighteousness" (John 1:9 NASB).

I am thankful for that rock-hard granola bar that freed me from a hidden infection. I am even more thankful for the bumps in life that remind me to ask the Lord to search my soul.

To be saved and set free from all hidden sins are true blessings in disguise that help me live a consecrated life filled with joy unspeakable and full of glory.

Will you ask the Holy Spirit to search for hidden sin in your life?

Dear Lord, please search my heart every day and bring to light any hidden or pet sins I may be harboring. I repent and ask You to wash them away in the blood of the Lamb.

In Jesus's Name, Amen.

Power in the Blood:
Declining the Impotent Gospel

Julie Souza Bradley Lilly

In him we have redemption through his blood, the forgiveness of sins, in accordance with the riches of God's grace.

~Ephesians 1:7 NIV

Years ago, I had a conversation with someone about offensive words found in scripture. I am not talking about unwholesome language, but words like *sin, death, crucifixion, hell* and *the blood.*

Some congregations had postulated that cultured people are offended by the graphic nature of these words, and a more diluted and sanitized gospel began to emerge.

All have sinned and fallen short of the glory of God. We are all aware of our sin, whatever we choose to call it. We feel its weight and desperation.

For all have sinned and fall short of the glory of God, being justified freely by His [God's] grace through the redemption that is in Christ Jesus.

~Romans 3:23-24 NKJV

We are not saved by a diluted and impotent gospel. We are not saved by our good deeds, good thoughts, or crossed fingers.

We are saved by the death of the sinless Son of God, who died as the sacrifice for sin. We are saved by Jesus Christ's blood that was poured out for you and for me—the love of God that endured

11

scourging, insult and abandonment by the very ones He gave His life to save.

For the wages of sin is death, but the gift of God is eternal life in Christ Jesus our Lord.

~Romans 6:23 NKJV

The enemy hates the blood of Jesus Christ. The mere mention reminds him of his impending demise. To dilute the truth plays into his plan to silence the hope that calls out to us from the blood and the empty tomb.

The Gospel does offend, beloved. Its beautiful brutality is offensive to those who are still in love with their sin.

But for those suffocating in their sin who are desperate for rescue and devoid of hope, it is the breath of life and an extended, nail-scarred hand that reaches out to snatch them from hell.

~Julie Souza Bradley Lilly

The Gospel does offend, beloved. Its beautiful brutality is offensive to those who are still in love with their sin.

But for those suffocating in their sin who are desperate for rescue and devoid of hope, it is the breath of life and an extended, nail-scarred hand that reaches out to snatch them from hell.

I am not ashamed of the gospel of Christ, for it is the power of God to salvation for everyone who believes.

~Romans 1:16a NKJV

Share your salvation experience.

Father God, I decline any impotent gospel. Bring me back to Your complete and unvarnished truth. I embrace the work of the cross and the blood of Christ that saves mankind. Send me to the four corners of the earth to spread the Good News in its entirety. May I leave nothing out and no one behind.

In Jesus's Name, Amen.

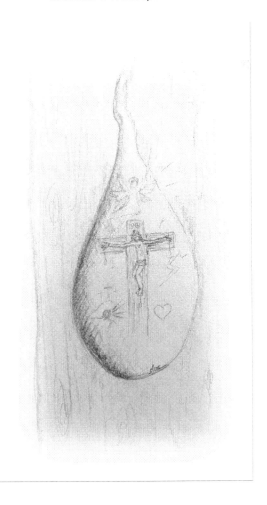

The "Messterpiece"

Shanda Neighbors

Whoever hears these sayings of Mine and does them, I will liken him to a wise man who built his house on a rock.

~Matthew 7:24b NKJV

I watched from the sidelines. It was supposed to be a team project. Parental involvement was not allowed.

The goal was stated simply enough: "Build a tower, as tall as possible, out of the designated amount of plastic drinking straws, paperclips, and masking tape." My daughter and her team huddled together. But the preteen girls were not conversing. Each member was doing her own thing.

From my vantage point, I could clearly see everything they were doing wrong. An unstable base. Zero support columns. Insufficient reinforcements.

The mama-urge to fix my child's problems was being challenged, and my competitive tendencies were also taking blows. Determined to be a good example, I did not intervene. I mostly watched. My only offering was encouraging them to speak to each other, but by the time they finally did, the other teams were further ahead, and some were even finished.

My daughter's team not only lost miserably, they managed to build what looked more like a straw squid than a tower. They dubbed it their "messterpiece."

"Messterpiece." Isn't that what we look like to God without His intervention? That very morning, I had awakened with Psalm 46:10 in mind, "Be still and know that I *am* God" (Psalm 46:10 NKJV).

The days before the competition had been crazy, and the previous night I had gone to bed feeling hopeless. There was so much weighing on me, I had felt overwhelmed. The anxiety was almost crippling.

In the midst of this trial, Psalm 46 arose in my spirit as nourishment. I abandoned everything to heed God's Word, and in my stillness, He gave me what I needed.

When tempted by the enemy through physical hunger, Jesus said, "Man shall not live by bread alone, but by every word that proceeds from the mouth of God" (Matt 4:4b NKJV). He said we should ask Him to give us our "daily bread," and He called Himself the "bread of life." The bread Jesus was speaking of was Himself. He is "The Word."

We need the Word to survive. We cannot make it on physical bread alone. Partaking in the Word is not a nice add-on or a suggestion for "good Christians." It is not the noble thing to do. It is a necessity and essential to our survival. Matthew 4:4b NKJV reads, "Man shall not live by bread alone, but by every word that proceeds from the mouth of God."

In John 6:66, Jesus told the Pharisees that unless they ate of His flesh and drank His blood, there was no life in them. It disturbed the audience. Understandably so, but Jesus wasn't talking about cannibalism. He was talking about the Word and the Spirit. The scriptures teach us that the Word of God is alive—that it became flesh." When we consume God's Word, it lives in us and gives life to us. Without it, we die in so many ways.

Truth be told, I had been living on the bread of my own wisdom and my own efforts. I was a "messterpiece" much like the girls' straw squid. I was supposed to be under the Master's construction, but I had taken projects into my own hands, and I was unstable. Struggling, my mind and body were going in many directions. It was utter confusion, just like the straw squid.

Thankfully, there was wisdom for me. Unlike the instruction my girls received, my Heavenly Father's involvement and wisdom are always needed. He may have given it sooner if I had asked Him, looked in the Word, and sought His direction.

Instead, I built first.

It wasn't until what I had constructed failed that I remembered to ask Him. Even then, it wasn't my "perfect repentance" that delivered me; it was His kindness, generosity, and truth that He alone possesses that made the difference within me.

God's Word is His communication to us.

If we listen and follow His lead, we will become the "masterpieces" He intends us to be.

~Shanda Neighbors

Jesus promised, "You will know the truth and the truth shall make you free" (John 8:32 NKJV). What is truth? Jesus is the Truth. Literally. He says, "I am the way, the truth, and the life" (John 14:6b NKJV).

A relationship with Truth is a relationship with the person, Jesus Christ. When we know Jesus, He makes us free. He did this for me, and He continues His work in me to this day.

As I stood watching the "messterpiece" being judged in the competition, the straw squid served as a visual reminder of not only what was, but what could have been if communication and adherence to wisdom had been employed. The girls had possessed all the pieces to build an effective structure.

There is no firmer foundation than God and His Word. There are no better plans than Jesus Christ's. Elevating our plans above His never works. His ways are perfect. My plans are "messterpieces" compared to His.

The girls were given a chance to explain their failed project. They shared that they had learned to communicate better and to choose a leader. This is a lesson we all need to learn.

God's Word is His communication to us. If we listen and follow His lead, we will become the "masterpieces" He intends us to be. If we do not, we will remain "messterpieces," sad reminders of what could have been.

Communication with God through His Word and prayer to Him is the blueprint for our lives. There are no other stable options.

Share a "messterpiece" turned "masterpiece" story of your own.

Father God, teach me to love You and regard Your Word, who we see revealed in the person of Jesus Christ, with high esteem. Let no activity nor person come before You. Give me the courage to lay aside my will. Help me to offer to You the reasonable sacrifice of a surrendered life. Build my character according to Your plans.

In Jesus's Name. Amen.

Psalm 18 Retold

Stephanie Pavlantos

He was in a fight for his life.

He knew who he was—he would be king. God chose him. But the reigning, evil ruler refused to give up his throne. He pursued the young ruddy shepherd to kill him. Saul wanted to show David who was stronger. David, however, was resilient and sharp. He knew where to hide and how to fight. After all, he had killed lions, bears, and even a giant. How could Saul overtake him?

But even would-be kings have moments of weakness.

David had had enough. He was tired of fighting, hiding, and running. He got weaker while Saul seemed to get stronger and more persistent. Believing his life was ending, David cried out to God.

God heard his cry. The earth rocked and quaked as lightning streaked across the sky. God's eyes glowed with fire and smoke rose from His nostrils. On a cherub, He thundered out of the heavens under a cover of darkness. Riding on the wind, every cloud parted as hailstones and arrows went before Him. As He broke through the sky, the brightness of His glory brought everything to light and exposed the earth.

He saw His beloved and gripped his hand as a sea of destruction threatened to take him over. He set David in a safe place away from his enemy.

Why? Because God delighted in him.

As fruit ripens on a branch before it is eaten, God was making David a righteous man. The shepherd who would be king kept the ways and laws of the LORD. He knew who he was and to whom he belonged. David's heart was in pursuit after the heart of God.

God is a God of magnificent character. He never changes. God is kindhearted, blameless, and pure. The Lord loves the humble and is light in our darkness.

As God's strength and righteousness surrounded him, David's fear left him. God replaced it with invincibility. He was feeling like himself again.

Bring on Saul's troops! There was no wall David could not leap over. As a buck's hooves balance him on mountain tops, David knew he could not stumble. God trained him for this war. Now he could bend a bow of bronze.

God is perfect. His Word is true. He is the shield which protects us. There is only one God, and He is our Rock. He saves us. As a mother wraps her arm around her toddler to keep him from falling, God supports us to make us great.

David could stand with God's power working in him. He was no longer the pursued, but the pursuer. David destroyed his enemies, and they did not rise again. He was no longer the one who feared, but he put the fear of the Lord in his adversaries. There was none to help them, no one to hear their cries. They were as dust in the wind, as mud on the road.

The conflict with his people disappeared. David became the head of nations, and people from all over revered and obeyed him. Strangers feared him because the power of his God was on him.

The LORD lives; blessed be my Rock and exalted is the God of my salvation. *

God gave David justice and conquered nations under him. He delivered him from his enemies and exalted him above those who sought to destroy him. The LORD rescued him from the man of violence.

David sang God's praises to all nations. God made him King. God showed His love to David and his descendants forever.

David... was no longer the pursued, but the pursuer.

~Stephanie Pavlantos

Put your name in David's place and read this again.

See the truth of what God will do for you. Although Satan opposes, he will not have his way. God will rush to you when you cry to Him.

Why? He delights in you!

God's nature is to rescue, love, protect, and restore. It's what He did for David, and He will do the same for you. God either fights our battles, or He strengthens us to fight. Even now He is training you how to win. With every battle you become stronger, and you lean more on your Savior and Rock.

You are the Lord's beloved.

Share three ways God has rescued you.

Heavenly Father, Thank You that I am Your beloved. You are great and worthy to be praised. I give You praise for rescuing me.

In Jesus's Name, Amen.

(Prose adapted from Psalm 18 ESV. * Psalm 118:46, adapted)

Tribulation in the Lab

Stephanie Pavlantos

So we can confidently say, "The Lord is my helper; I will not fear; what can man do to me?"

~Hebrews 13:6 ESV

At twenty-five-years-old, I had a stomach ulcer from the stress of my job.

I had found a laboratory that would hire an inexperienced college graduate with a B.S. in biology. The VA hospital needed a histology technician, and they were willing to train me to do the job. Histologists make slides from the tissue removed from the body during surgery, which pathologists review to make a diagnosis for the patient.

I came, excited to learn.

I did not realize I was about to learn more than histology. God was about to throw me into the middle of a spiritual battle....

My supervisor did not like me from the first day. She criticized my work clothes, my hairstyle, and the fact that I wore contact lenses. She demanded I pull back my hair and wear glasses. Good thing I wasn't there to find a boyfriend—it would have never happened. She thought I flirted with the doctors who came into our lab when I simply acknowledged their presence.

It got worse.

She did not allow me to take some of my breaks, and if she wanted me back in the lab before lunch was over, she would stage a phone call from a "family member," who mysteriously hung up before I got to the phone. Equipment from my locker began to disappear after she watched me stow it away for the night. I was not free from her even at home because she would call if I took the day off. I was too demoralized to complain, and I felt I was being held hostage by fear and intimidation.

I cried to the Lord every day.

Although discouragement and hopelessness were my constant companions, I sensed God's presence in the midst of it all. The Lord met with me each morning as I worshipped, and as I poured out my heart, and He filled my soul.

The Lord surrounded me with friends who taught me to pray against the forces of spiritual darkness.

~Stephanie Pavlantos

As I grew in faith and dependence on my Savior, I sensed God would work good out of this difficult situation. However, the more I grew in my faith, the worse the harassment became.

The Lord surrounded me with friends who taught me to pray against the forces of spiritual darkness that had control of my supervisor. I knew the Lord was with me.

After a year, I interviewed for another job at the hospital. They offered me the position, but I sensed the Lord did not want me to take that job. Saddened, I turned it down, but God gave me immediate peace.

After working in the Histology Department for two years, the head lab manager gave me a significant pay raise and promotion because of my qualifications. My supervisor, who had no control over this promotion, was furious. She increased the attacks, wanting to prove I was undeserving of this preferment.

Hebrews 13:5b ESV became my anchor, "For he has said, 'I will never leave you nor forsake you.'"

I begged God to let me leave. Finally, He did.

The Lord had an incredible job waiting for me in the Cancer Research Department. The requirements? They were looking for a histologist with two years of lab experience.

If I had taken my eyes off of Jesus and surrendered to the hopelessness of my circumstances, I would have missed out on a job I loved.

Friend, no matter what situation you are in—whether a bad relationship, a difficult job, or a health challenge—don't give up.

Keep your eyes on Jesus Christ, and hold on to your faith. Trust Him to guide you every step of the way. God has you in the palm of His hand and He is with you. He is your constant companion in good times and in bad, and He will see you through.

Share ways the Lord has worked His will despite difficult curcumstances.

Heavenly Father, You've promised to never to leave me nor forsake me. I trust and acknowledge You are good, even when I don't understand how You will work Your will for my good, despite tough times. I choose to praise and thank You in all circumstances. I love You, and I receive Your great love for me.

In Jesus's Name, Amen.

#

Glenda Shouse

Let everything that has breath praise the Lord.

~Psalm 150:6 NKJV

I was having a "woe-is-me" day, recounting all the problems in my life.

Can you remember having a day when you counted "woes" instead of blessings?

The enemy of our soul is happy when we are distracted by the trials we are experiencing. His tactic is to distract us with negative thoughts so we won't notice God's goodness and beauty surrounding us.

On this beautiful sunny "woe-counting" day, I drove to the backwaters of a lake. My mind was on me and all I needed to accomplish instead of remembering all Jesus had done for me.

But then, I noticed a log sticking out of the water. Lined up on the log was a row of turtles with their heads raised high. They were basking in the sun and appeared to be praising the Lord. These lovely little creations of God instinctively knew what to do.

What a wonderful reminder it was to me that all creation praises God.

In Psalm 103 we read, "Bless the Lord, all His works, in all places of His dominion. Bless the Lord, O my soul." Look around you. No matter the circumstances of your life, open your eyes to see God's good works. And then praise Him.

My circumstances did not change on my "woe-is-me" day, but my heart did as I began praising the Lord for His goodness.

~Glenda Shouse

Remember, friend, you are loved by the One who created everything for His good pleasure. He uses everything in our lives for good so we will see Him clearly, whether it is the moments we fail to be obedient, or the times we follow Him closely.

The Psalmist says, "Bless the Lord, all His works, in all places of His dominion. Bless the Lord, O my soul" (Psalm 103:22 NKJV). My circumstances did not change on my "woe-is-me" day, but my heart did as I began praising the Lord for His goodness. God invites you to praise Him too.

Share three ways you can re-focus your thoughts on God when you are experiencing a "woe is me" day.

Lord Jesus, thank You for the breath You give me. Enable me to praise You with everything that is within me no matter how I am feeling. Empower me to give You glory in all circumstances.

Amen.

25

The Perfect Cake

Glenda Shouse

See what great love the Father has lavished on us, that we should be called children of God! And that is what we are! The reason the world does not know us is that it did not know him.

~1 John 3:1 NIV

Mmmmm...

That bowl of butter-cream icing looks yummy. It is ready to be lavished onto three perfect cake layers.

Oh, wait a minute. They're not perfect.

One cake is split, and another has a missing piece that stuck to the pan. However, once I lavish them with this luscious topping, they will look beautiful.

Just like the icing smooths out the imperfections of the cakes, we look to our Heavenly Father to perfect us as He lavishes His love upon us. His love covers our imperfections until all that can be seen is the beauty of Jesus Christ within us.

Lavish! 1 John 3:1 references this rich word. Father God lavishes us with His love because we are His beloved children. He knows and cherishes us.

I am also reminded of Mary of Bethany who lavished the head of Jesus with the most costly posession she owned—she donned Her Savior's crown with the perfumed oil of her dowry. She did not hold back. Instead she gave the Lord her most treasured possession.

Mark 14:3 NKJV reads, "And being in Bethany at the house of Simon the leper, as He [Jesus] sat at the table, a woman came having an alabaster flask of very costly oil of spikenard. Then she broke the flask and poured *it* on His head."

As Mary broke this flask, she demonstrated lavish love. In contrast, some people around her whispered about her act, accusing her as being wasteful of a precious commodity.

But Jesus received Mary of Bethany's lavish love, and He said her sacrificial love would be remembered. We still do remember her lavish love, and her story is recorded in three of the four Gospels.

Father God ... continually pours His lavish love on us, in us, and through us.

~Glenda Shouse

Let's define "lavish."

It means to give something in profusion, or in great amounts, or without limits. Don't you just love this word?

Lavish! Say it and see how it feels in your mouth. Just like the lovely cake, this word almost makes your mouth water. It is so rich. It's like tasting the icing on the spatula you used to ice the cake.

Step into the world of imagination.

Take more than a sample spoonful of the word "lavish." Don't be satisfied to taste a sample. Fill your mouth with this word, "lavish." Why? Father God has a limitless supply of His lavish love and He has lavished us with more love than we can imagine.

Lavish love is what our Heavenly Father gives to us, simply because we are His children. He continually pours His lavish love on us, in us, and through us. He fills us to overflowing, and with the help of the Holy Spirit, we can share His love with everyone around us.

Let's make it our heart's desire to pour love on our family, friends, and others we may encounter as we go about our day. We want everyone in our sphere of influence to know we love them. The love we share is a small sampling of the enormous love the Father has for them, so He entrusts us to be His representatives.

Not only does Father God lavish His love on us and through us, He also lavishes us with unlimited grace.

Paul shares, "In Him we have redemption through his blood, the forgiveness of sins, in accordance with the riches of God's grace that He lavished on us with all wisdom and understanding" (Ephesians 1:7-8 NIV).

What a marvelous Father we have! He covers us and fills us with His love and grace. His love is like a delicious cake.

"Taste and see that the Lord is good; blessed is the one who takes refuge in him" (Psalm 34:8 NIV).

Share a circumstance where you've experienced God's lavish love.

Father God, I receive the lavish love and grace You pour into my life. Help me to be Your representative, sharing this with others wherever You send me.

In Jesus's Name, Amen.

Why Choose Faith in God?

Sandra Stein

Start children off in the way they should go, and even when they are old, they will not turn from it.

~Proverbs 22:6 NIV

Faith... I had every reason not to believe.

But God had a different path for me. He saw my pain, and He rescued me when circumstances would have destroyed every ounce of belief I could have mustered.

The reason why I chose faith in God and in His Son Jesus Christ—even when every outward circumstance dictated I should not—may not have made sense, but within my spirit, it felt completely right.

The dictionary defines faith as having complete trust or confidence in someone or in something, or a strong belief in God, or having religious beliefs that are based on spiritual apprehension rather than on proof.

The "something" part of this definition is easy. I put faith in a lot of things—my car starting, my washing machine turning on, and my alarm clock waking me. If they fail to perform, I run to the store, the mechanic, or a service professional.

But putting faith in "someone?" I didn't want to go there. That was a new level of trust. Betrayal was my normal experience, so I did not know how to put my trust in any person, let alone God whom I could not see.

My parents did not raise me in church. If you asked me as a seven-year-old what church was, I'd scratch my head and reply I had no idea. But that changed when I met a woman named Mrs. Adams who had great faith—the kind of faith Paul writes about, "So then faith comes by hearing, and hearing by the Word of God" (Romans 10:17 NKJV).

I admired Mrs. Adams. She made me feel secure.

Mrs. Adams invited the neighborhood kids to her home. She called the group Missionettes, and she taught us in a school-like setting. We made crafts, sang songs, and learned about God.

The only time I had heard Jesus's name prior to meeting Mrs. Adams was when my dad yelled it in a nasty way. But Mrs. Adams spoke Jesus's name in reverence. I could tell she adored Him more than I adored her.

I did not understand why, but even though what I experienced at Mrs. Adam's home was unlike what I experienced at my home, I had an inner nudge that assured me I belonged in this place.

Mrs. Adams taught us God's Son was Jesus Christ. She told us we could talk to God and Jesus anytime through prayer. I felt content in this environment. When Mrs. Adams told us that to have effective prayers, we needed to put our faith in God, I was intrigued but hesitant.

Dare I get that close to God?

Faith?

A complete trust or confidence in "Someone?" I wasn't sure.

As a child growing up in an abusive home and surviving the hatred of my dad and the horrible things he did to me, I felt I could not put faith in anyone. The circumstances I was living in gave me no reason to want to believe. Why should I put my faith in a God no one could prove existed?

Scripture states, "Be strong and courageous. Do not be afraid or terrified because of them, for the Lord your God goes with you; he will never leave you nor forsake you (Deuteronomy 31:6 NIV). I would learn this much later. At the time, I was relying on Mrs. Adams's faith in Jesus Christ as she demonstrated His trustworthiness.

Though I was hesitant, Mrs. Adams's teachings about God's love started to take root in my mind and spirit. The words, "God loves you," resonated peace within my inner being.

Finally, I decided to pray.

I told God how scared I was about everything that was happening in my home, and how alone I felt. The more I prayed, the more my fears subsided. I asked God's Son, Jesus Christ, to be my Savior. I did not want to just know about Him; I wanted to receive Him as mine, and have a relationship with Him, like Mrs. Adams.

Before putting faith in God, my life was terrifying, but after my faith-experience, I had a reason to live.

~Sandra Stein

The next day I woke up with a smile on my face for the first time.

Through my prayers, and as I heard other Bible verses, the truth about God and Jesus Christ became real to me over time. I realized God was alive, and He truly did love me.

I had an inner peace I could not describe.

Before putting faith in God, my life was terrifying, but after my faith-experience, I had a reason to live.

I put my faith in God for three reasons: 1) God loved me when others would not. 2) He was there for me. 3) He gave me something no one else offered—peace, comfort, and joy.

Over time, my faith has grown tremendously. God's promises are true, and they are for you as much as they are for me.

What do I believe? The Bible tells us God sent His only Son Jesus to die on a cross and bear the death penalty of our sins, so we can be forgiven. Jesus was conceived by the Holy Spirit, and born through the virgin Mary, and therefore He was the perfect God-Man. This qualified Him to die in our place as the perfect substitute for sin. He is alive, having been raised from the dead, victorious over death, hell, and the grave. Jesus ascended into heaven. He is coming again, and for those who put their faith in Him, He will take us to live with Him in heaven for all of eternity. Our job here is to trust Jesus Christ as our Savior, and to share this Good News with others.

I can testify that asking Jesus Christ to be your Savior is the best decision you can ever make. Take the step of faith and put your trust in Him today.

Have you asked Jesus Christ to be your Savior?

Heavenly Father, I choose to put my faith in You and I accept Your Son, Jesus Christ, as my personal Savior and Lord. Help me to trust the promises in the Bible, and to grow in my faith every day.

In Jesus's Name, Amen.

My Superhero

Diane Virginia

Now to the King eternal, immortal, invisible, to God who alone is wise, be honor and glory forever and ever. Amen.

~1 Timothy 1:17 NKJV

I smelled rubber as the sedan screeched to a halt.

With legs sprawled and palms outstretched, my three-year-old son stood in front of the car with an expression of delight.

How had he slipped his hand out of mine?

I scooped my son into my arm, tightened my grip on my daughter's hand, and apologized to the driver.

Once inside the store, I asked, "Son, what were you thinking?"

"I'm Superman! I stop car!" My son flexed his muscles to demonstrate his power.

"Mom, that was neat," my daughter said, her innocent eyes adoring her brother's courageous act.

"Not exactly," I said, making a mental note to discuss street safety later that evening. *I'll shelve the Superhero videos for now*, I thought, but I knew that would be futile.

To my three-and-four-year-old children, superheroes were as real as Charlotte, the spider who lived on the porch, and I was not permitted to sweep her web away in case she wanted to write them a message. The Easter Bunny lived in the neighborhood—my children had seen him. Sure enough, Gilligan would teach my children boating skills—as soon as he found a way off the island. Mr. Rogers would bring Lady Elaine and Daniel for a visit soon. My children were sure this was true because he liked them just the way they were.

Superheroes empower children.

With their imaginations activated, they can envision the world as a safe place to grow, learn, and play.

Once we become adults, we lose that safety-net of knowing there is a superpower greater than ourselves...or do we? With faith activated, we can know the One who is more majestic than any imaginary superhero, whose Name is mightier than any name that is named.

With faith activated, we can know the One who is more majestic than any imaginary Superhero, whose Name is mightier than any name that is named.

~Diane Virginia

Are you looking for a superhero? Look no farther than Jesus Christ.

He is the Superhero who carries our fears, so we don't have to. He is the One who activates dreams—even those we gave up on ever achieving. He heals the body that aches when the doctors have been unable to find the ailment or the cure. He breathes life into the lost soul whose wounds are masked behind addictions. He speaks peace to the man who feels rejected. He reinstates the marriage that is shredding apart day-by-day, as couples grasp for dying love. Jesus

Christ is the One who provides bread on our table when the mortgage is due and dollars are few.

In 1 Timothy, Paul pens a picture of our Superhero, "Christ Jesus came into the world to save sinners; of whom I am chief" (1 Timothy 1:15b NKJV).

How could Paul pen these words with such conviction, and state his own personal failure without flinching? Even though Paul had committed great sins, he had experienced Christ's transforming power.

I like that, because it lets us know our Superhero Jesus Christ extends forgiveness to all those who call upon His Name.

This is why Paul writes two verses later, this memorable praise, "Now to the King eternal, immortal, invisible, to God who alone is wise, *be* honor and glory forever and ever. Amen" (1 Timothy 1:17 NKJV).

How can we thank our Superhero Jesus Christ as eloquently as Paul? Even though we are adults, God has placed within us the indelible gift of imagination. As we pray, we can envision with child-like faith just how majestic our real-life Superhero truly is, all the while knowing that even our best attempt at this cannot fully reveal the complete majesty of our Savior.

Jesus Christ. He is the Superhero we all need.

Share a character trait about your Superhero Jesus Christ.

Heavenly Father, help me to envision my real-life Superhero Jesus Christ in His majesty and splendor.

In Jesus's Name, Amen.

The Speeding Ticket

Diane Virginia

Casting all your care upon Him: for He cares for you.

~1 Peter 5:7 NKJV

The reflection of blue lights flashed in my rear-view mirror. Embarrassed, I pulled over.

"Ma'am, can you explain why you were speeding?"

"I... waaasn't paying attention," I stammered.

I understood that not knowing my speed was not an excuse. I was responsible for operating my vehicle safely.

The officer ticketed me, and I went my way.

When I got home, I looked at the ticket. Fifty-four miles per hour in a forty-five mile per hour zone was a serious infraction. I researched the potential consequences: one-year revocation of license, lawyer costs, court costs, insurance points. I felt nauseous. Rather than worrying further, I bowed my head and released the situation I was responsible for into God's mighty hands.

"Father, You gave me the license, so it is Yours to take or to give as You desire. I surrender this situation to You."

I called my husband, and he called our attorney.

"I can possibly get the charges reduced by ten miles per hour," the lawyer said, "or, if we're lucky, the charges could be reduced to 'improper equipment.'" He went on to explain his rates, court costs, and potential insurance rate hikes. "Do you have questions I can help you with? And try not to worry about this. I'll do my best to get this matter resolved."

"When I go to court, will you be with me?"

"No."

"What?" My face flushed as I thought about standing in front of the judge. Alone.

"I am going in your place."

"What did you say?" I pressed my abdomen, hoping it would calm down.

"You are to stay home. I will speak to the judge on your behalf. I will function as your representative."

"Thank you, sir."

A few days later, my lawyer called. "Your case has been dismissed."

"Dismissed? As in forgiven?" I was shocked.

"Not exactly. It's better than that."

"Better than forgiven?"

"That's right. Dismissed means we are acting as if this incident never happened. It will not appear on your record, you owe no court costs, and this will not be reported to your insurance company. Your slate is wiped clean."

"Wiped clean?"

"Yes. Wiped clean. Completely."

"Thank you! How can I ever repay you?"

"I don't expect you to. Oh, and by the way, my services are gratis."

"Gratis?"

"That's right; you owe me nothing. Not a penny."

"Not a penny? That's almost too good to be true. May I ask why?"

"Let's just say, you have a reputation."

"Are you sure?"

"I'm positive. Have a nice day."

The next morning, the Scripture I read during my quiet time was, "For Thou, Lord, art good, and ready to forgive; and plenteous in mercy unto all them that call upon thee" (Psalm 86:5 KJV).

God is good, and even if my license had been revoked, I would still have reason to believe this is true. Father God loves us so much He sent His Son Jesus to die in our place and to take the punishment for our transgressions—even the ones that are more serious than traffic violations.

Every way we've messed up, Jesus Christ has already paid for.

Father God has made it possible, through belief in His Son, Jesus, for our record of sins to be wiped away.

Colossians 2:14 KJV reads, "Blotting the handwriting of ordinances that was against us, which was contrary to us, and took it out of the way, nailing it to his cross."

Jesus Christ erased the charges that were against us with His own shed blood. It is as if we have never sinned, even though we were the guilty ones. The work Jesus accomplished in Calvary's cross was beyond forgiveness; the charges against us have been dismissed.

When I get to heaven, no one will say, "Remember when you were speeding?" Not only was I forgiven, I—the guilty one—was re-made, as if I had never sinned. The same goes for each of us who call upon His Name.

When we give our mistakes to Jesus, He blots out the transgressions as if the situations never happened at all.

The work Jesus Christ accomplished on Calvary's cross was beyond forgiveness; the charges against us have been dismissed.

~Diane Virginia

We read in 2 Corinthians 5:17b NLV, "Anyone who belongs to Christ has become a new person. The old life is gone; a new life has begun!" We are renewed through the shed blood of Jesus Christ.

Our good God knew we would need a Savior, so He sent the finest Lawyer to represent us that mankind we could ever dream about. Jesus Christ cares about every detail of our lives, and His representation is the best ever.

Share an experience where God intervened, wiping your record of transgressions clean.

Thank You, God, for sending Jesus Christ to wipe my record clean.

In Jesus's Name, Amen.

Lessons in Faith

Evelyn Wells

Now faith is the assurance of things hoped for, the conviction of things not seen.

~Hebrews 11:1 ESV

In the Book of Daniel, we read about four friends who exemplified outstanding faith. How so? They had complete assurance in God, even without the certainty of the outcomes of life-or-death situations they would face.

Perhaps this clues you as to their identity. They are Daniel and his friends Hanaiah, Mishael, and Azariah. We are more familiar with the names King Nebuchadnezzar gave them—Belteshazzar, Shadrach, Meshach, and Abednego. Daniel and his friends went through three years of training in order to serve King Nebuchadnezzar of Babylon, who had enslaved them.

Shadrach, Meshach, and Abednego demonstrated faith in God even when they were thrown into a fiery furnace. They refused to bow to the king's false god and worship it, even if it cost them their lives. Though they weren't sure God would save them, they still trusted Him. They knew God saw the big picture and their place in it.

They also knew that the one true God is faithful. Dead or alive, they were in His hands. Therefore, they said to the King, "If we are thrown into the blazing furnace, the God we serve is able to deliver us from it, and he will deliver us from Your Majesty's hand. But even if he does not, we want you to know, Your Majesty, that we will not serve your gods or worship the image of gold you have set up" (Daniel 3:16b-18 NIV).

When the heat subsided, the king looked into the furnace. Although the fire was still burning, and he did not expect to see anyone alive, he not only saw the three who were cast into the furnace—he saw a fourth man walking with Daniel's friends.

Who was this Fourth Man? King Nebuchadnezzar recognized he was in the presence of a deity. He stated the Fourth Man looked like a Son of God. We know this Man as Jesus Christ.

Daniel also demonstrated great faith. When King Darius conquered Babylon, he exalted himself, proclaiming to be a god. He established a new ordinance that instructed everyone to bow down and worship only him. The consequence for disobedience was that they would be thrown into the lion's den.

Because of Daniel's deep faith, he continued to bow and worship to God every day during his prayer time.

Furthermore, Daniel made no secret of his commitment to serve the Lord, and only Him.

As would be expected, Daniel was cast in the lions' den.

Daniel was willing to die, but the king was unable to harm him because God shut the mouths of the lions. When King Darius looked into the den and saw that Daniel was untouched by the ravaging beasts, he was shocked.

As a result, the king put his trust in Daniel's God.

The Book of Daniel shows us that sometimes it takes more than a faith-statement to prove our faithfulness to God. He may ask us to put our lives on the line.

If God would require us, would we be willing to display the extraordinary faith of these four heroes? Daniel, Shadrach, Meshach, and Abednego were not superhuman, but they were committed to

God in an extrodinary way. They were willing to be used by God in whatever way He desired, even if it meant they would die for Him.

Because of this, God used them to prove His great power.

What if we demonstrated faith like these heroes had? These men had faith that changes lives, to the point of even affecting kings and kingdoms. I want life-changing faith, too. Whether or not we are asked to die for Him, the fact remains that Jesus died for us.

Whether or not we are asked to die for Him, the fact remains that Jesus died for us.

~Evelyn Wells

Our faith is not meant to be confined behind the walls of the church. God asks us to share the Good News not only in our churches, but also in our workplaces, amongst our friends, on the mission field, and wherever God directs us.

The Lord calls us to a life of faith in our ever-present Lord, Jesus Christ. Let's make the decision to have the commitment of these four heroes of faith.

Share three ways that living a life of faith can affect others.

Thank You, Father in heaven, for Your love, mercy, and grace. Through Your Son, Jesus Christ, You have provided a way for me to be confident in my faith. Help me to be committed to You in the extrodinary way Daniel, Shadrach, Meshach, and Abednigo were.

In Jesus's Name, Amen.

Taking the Chastisement

Martin Wiles

For the Lord disciplines those he loves, and he punishes each one he accepts as his child.

~Hebrews 12:6 NLT

She knew what she'd done—and took her punishment willingly.

Our little Chihuahua-terrier mix has a sweet tooth. After many episodes of her getting into candy, suckers, and chocolate of various types, we learned to put away the trash can, shut doors, and remove any candy within her reach while we were away.

But one Valentine's Day, we forgot.

Our oldest grandson's teacher had given a Valentine party for the students in her class. Levi came home with a large bag full of candy, which he placed on the floor by my wife's recliner. When the phone rang, telling us my wife's car was ready at the repair shop, we all piled into my old car and headed to get it.

When we returned and walked into the house, Rita lay crouched by my wife's recliner. Since she sometimes greets us that way, I thought nothing of it—until I walked into the den. On the floor lay an empty box of conversational hearts, or what was left of it. The box top had been torn off and a few hearts lay scattered about. The rest were in Rita's stomach.

"Riiiita," I said in the most chiding voice I could muster. (I'm not too good at scolding her, since she's my little lap dog and spoiled to boot.) She laid her ears back and cowered a little lower, but remained where she was.

"Riiiita." My wife's booming voice brought a different reaction. Rita scurried to the bedroom and scooted into her kennel—and stayed without the gate latched. "She knows what to do when she's in trouble," my wife said.

After a few minutes—when I thought she had learned her lesson, even though I knew better—I said, "Rita, you can come out now." And she did, with her tail wagging and her tongue going.

God disciplines because we are His children, and He loves us ...

Take God's chastening with a good spirit.

~Martin Wiles

I've never enjoyed punishing any animal I've ever owned, but I know it's necessary if they are to learn what they should and should not do. I consider it more training than discipline, although that's what discipline is.

God disciplines because we are His children, and He loves us—just as my parents disciplined me because I belonged to them, and they were responsible for my behavior. "But consider the joy of those corrected by God! Do not despise the discipline of the Almighty when you sin" (Job 5:17 NLT).

I'll be the first to admit I don't much like God's chiding—and sometimes, like my dog, I crouch down when I know it's coming. But occasionally, I'll do what she did: take it like a man because I know God has my best interests at heart. I'll crouch a little lower because I know I've done wrong and then willingly go to my kennel—or wherever God sends me—until He sets me free, which is when He knows I've learned my lesson...at least for the moment.

Rita doesn't get into trouble nearly as much as she once did. She has tired of the kennel and of the gentle pops on her rear end or nose. She also knows she's less likely to get treats when she breaks the rules. As she has gotten older, the lessons have stuck—not entirely, but more than they once did. Wisdom comes with age. And not only for dogs.

When you get off track—or eat what you're not supposed to—take God's chastening with a good spirit. After all, He does it with love and for your own good.

How do you react when God disciplines you?

Father God, thank You for caring for me through disciplinary measures.

In Jesus's Name, Amen

Family

Family Founded in Love

Diane Virginia

Sisters we are, though not of blood,

God set His hand upon us, then tied a chord of love,

An enduring friendship, our adoption is truer than true,

As the voice of Naomi to Ruth erases life's rue.

Husband of mine, once enticed by romance,

Strengthened through trials and joys, as a synchronized dance,

Hand-in-hand we navigate the maze,

As God's unseen hand unites us and sets our spirits ablaze.

Son-of-our-heart, son and daughter of blood,

You fill our family with accomplishments and love,

As you lean on our family to compete in this game called Life,

Though the wisdom we offer is seldom complete.

Four-footed family, you've stilled our worried paces,

Through slobbery kisses and tennis ball races,

But more often than not, it's your eyes ablue,

and your paw that nudges, that see us through.

God of heaven, You've adopted our family,

Through Your Son, who paid sin's price in finality,

That our family bond may be founded in You,

And that through Christ's love, You will make us new.

What's in Your Garden?

Ed Chappelle

Therefore, rid yourselves of all malice and all deceit, hypocrisy, envy, and slander of every kind. Like newborn babies, crave pure spiritual milk, so that by it you may grow up in your salvation, now that you have tasted that the Lord is good.

~1 Peter 2:1-3 NIV

I balanced on the exam room table, bent at the waist, head down. My wife Kym held my hand. We were bracing for the inevitable but unwelcomed diagnosis....

"You have Type 2 diabetes," the doctor said matter-of-factly.

I felt gut-punched.

Even though I knew this diagnosis was coming, the doctor's words made it a reality to me. He went through some paperwork, which I tried to concentrate on, but I knew what I must do. The doctor exited, and we made our way to the check-out counter.

"We need to go home and clean house," I said to Kym. "Every piece of junk food in our pantry is going in the trash. We have got to get rid of all of it and adjust how we think about eating."

"Let's check the fridge too," Kym said with a wince. She had just made me a goodie, but she and I both knew it was going to be trashed with the rest of the goodies.

Although not all diabetes is due to food choices, I knew that in my case this was a contributing factor. I needed to make a change, and I was eager to do so.

49

I was also aware this was a family matter, and that because I could count on Kym's support, I would succeed. I viewed Kym's support as my greatest blessing.

I looked at my wife. Her eyes were brimming with tears. My resolve was firm. I had to do this—for her.

One decision Kym and I made after we cleaned our fridge was to start shopping from our local produce stand. We needed to replace junk food with the real stuff.

Garden-fresh produce could give my body and hers the nourishment they craved. We needed to be purposeful in what we allowed to enter our bodies, and this would start by choosing the best foods available to us and only permitting these into our house.

In Peter 2:1-3, the disciple talks about cleaning house in the spiritual realm. But instead of food needing a look-over, he tells us to adjust our attitudes. Peter says we must get rid of malice, deceit, hypocrisy, envy, and slander.

Wow! That's a tall order.

How do we make this adjustment effectively? Peter instructs us to replace these with "pure spiritual milk." With this, he references the Bible.

We need to prioritize reading our Bibles. This needs to be a deliberate choice of our will. A baby cannot go without milk, and in the spiritual realm, and neither can we deprive our spirits. God gives us fundamental truths—spiritual "milk"—as our starting place to build a strong spiritual home.

We need to make sure we are harvesting good fruits from our spiritual gardens and uprooting bad fruits. We need to tend our spiritual gardens by pulling up weeds of doubt, fear, and disbelief, as well as those Peter mentioned—malice, deceit, hypocrisy, envy, and slander. All harmful attitudes must be trashed.

The enemy of our souls is constantly trying to sow these bad fruits into our gardens. Therefore, we must be watchful, and continuously tend our gardens, so our faith in God can strengthen.

We need to tend our spiritual gardens by pulling up the weeds of doubt, fear, and disbelief, as well as those Peter mentioned—malice, deceit, hypocrisy, envy, and slander. All harmful attitudes must be trashed.

~Ed Chappelle

Just as I must watch the foods I consume, spiritual care must be intentional. Being consistent and committed would be a key to my success.

If I had gone home and paid no attention to the doctor's advice to learn to conquer the diabetic disease that had come upon me, then it could have caused havoc on my physical body.

It is the same in the spiritual realm; intentionality is essential.

Paul's solution is readily available to us. Our Bibles serve as milk, which is nourishment to our spirits. We start there, and then we read some more, learning to know the Bible in every intricacy.

Intentionality goes on to produce good fruits. Paul writes, "But the fruit of the Spirit is love, joy, peace, patience, kindness, goodness, faithfulness, gentleness, and self-control" (Galatians 5:22 NIV).

We study more until we are eating the "meat" of God's Word along with the milk, as well as every spiritual fruit God has made available to us. We become satiated with the fundamental truths as well as the deeper truths of our faith.

Just as I have begun my journey of learning how to eat well, so must we hear, read, and consume the truths in God's Word as the best sustenance.

What's more, God comes alongside to help us every step of our journey. I have committed to grow spiritually healthy, and my wife Kym supports this decision, too. In fact, we are journeying in our faith-walk together.

Name a family member who supports your healthy faith choices?

Heavenly Father, help me to examine my spiritual garden. I desire to get rid of anything that causes my relationship with You to suffer. Thank You for giving me the milk, fruit, and meat of the Word as nourishment to my spirit. Thank You also for giving Your Son, Jesus Christ, in whom I have everlasting life.

In Jesus's Name, Amen.

Prioritizing the Diamond

Amanda Eldridge

For where your treasure is, there your heart will be also.

~Matthew 6:21b NASB

I recently did an activity with my kids. I asked them to write down the most valuable things to them—those they treasure. I laid out jewel-colored construction paper for them to write on that represented jewels. Blue represented sapphire. Green was for emerald. Red was for ruby. I saved the white to represent the diamond which they were not allowed to write on at first.

My children got busy right away. They wrote "Mama" and "Daddy" on the green-emerald colored paper, "Nana" and "Mamaw" on the ruby-red paper, and "Uncle Josh" and "Aunt Bonnie" on the blue-sapphire paper. Then they wrote more names of other family and friends on the colored paper, as well as some of their favorite things, like art, nature, and food. They also decided to write God and Jesus on a color of their choice.

We talked about other things we should consider to be valuable that we don't always recognize, like time, energy, and resources. We listed these intangible items.

When the list was complete, I pulled out the white paper. In the center, I wrote "God." He is the "Diamond" because He is the most valuable of all gems.

From there, we talked about what is of value in our relationship with Him, like prayer, worship, reading the Bible, loving others, and so on.

It was a fun lesson. I felt it taught me more than it did my children.

I became curious and began to research information on diamonds. I discovered ways to determine if a diamond is fake or real. One way to discern this is to look for the rainbow coloration.

If we can see rainbow colors inside of a diamond, it is fake.

Interestingly though, if the diamond is real, it reflects rainbow colors onto surfaces rather than within it.

For me, this was a revelation.

If God truly is the most precious and valuable person in our lives, His love and light will flow through us, reflecting onto those valuable things around us.

~Amanda Eldridge

The colors of the rainbow are like the jeweled colors of our lives. The reds, blues, and greens of precious and semi-precious stones represent people, places, and possessions that we love. But if they become a god to us, we are focusing on a false god, just like we can have a fake diamond we think is real.

If God truly is the most precious and valuable person in our lives, His love and light will flow through us, and reflect onto those valuable things around us.

There is a reason God made diamonds hard to find. I am reminded of two Scriptures:

- "*It is* the glory of God to conceal a matter, but the glory of kings *is* to search out a matter" (Proverbs 25:2 NKJV).
- "In him lie hidden all the treasures of wisdom and knowledge" (Colossians 2:3 NKJV).

When we place value and honor on God and our relationship with Him, we don't take the easy way out. Instead, we make time for Him.

We pray. We read. We seek.

I have decided to start asking myself regularly, "Where is your heart?"

Will you seek the Lord with me and prioritize the Diamond who is the greatest treasure in our lives? Where our heart is, there will our treasure be as well.

What is one way you can prioritize God in your life?

Heavenly Father, thank You for being my genuine Diamond—superior above all other gems—and for being the treasure of my heart.
Help me to prioritize You.

In Jesus's Name, Amen.

Can God Heal Family Pets?

Karen Jurgens

In his hand is the life of every creature and the breath of all mankind.

~Job 12:10 NIV

I felt a paw scratch at my leg. I closed my book and looked down at Bo, our family's black toy poodle. "What do you want, sweet pea?" I set aside my popcorn.

At first, I assumed he was begging for a bite of my snack, but his soft whine and tense body language insisted that wasn't the case. My mind lit up with concern.

Bending over, I picked him up and held him close. "What's wrong?" I whispered in his ear.

His shallow breaths sounded raspy. His sides moved like an accordion as he tried to inhale. His chocolate eyes pleaded for me to do something.

My concern deepened. I knew all about asthma in people---but could a dog also have it?

Jesus, what should I do?

I cradled him in my arms and walked outside, hoping some fresh air would help.

It didn't.

My parents arrived home shortly thereafter, and I was relieved to hand Bo over to my mother for her expert care. Both of my parents expressed alarm at his condition.

"We're taking this dog to Dr. Sanders first thing tomorrow," Mother decided.

Early that next day, I was anxious to see if Bo had improved. From the worry etched under my parents' eyes, I saw the answer without asking. His little body was still trying to suck in oxygen through his raspy throat, and he looked exhausted and miserable.

My parents wrapped him in a light blanket and headed out the door.

"Call me with any news." Tears formed in the corners of my eyes. I ran to my room and picked up my Bible to searched scriptures about healing. I meditated on Matthew 9:35 NKJV, "Then Jesus went about all the cities and villages, teaching in their synagogues, preaching the gospel of the kingdom, and healing every sickness and every disease among the people."

Lord, I don't see any scriptures about healing animals, but if You do, please have mercy on Bo. Please, please heal our sweet poodle.

An hour later, I heard my parents walk through the door. I put down my Bible and rounded a corner, hoping to see Bo happy and back to normal—surely the vet had fixed him up with a shot or pills. But their arms were empty.

Alarm pierced me like a knife. "Where's the dog? Outside?"

A tear trickled down Mother's face.

My father frowned, studying the Mexican tile floor.

A hard knot twisted my stomach, and my heart skipped a beat. "Where is he?" My voice trembled.

My father placed a kind hand on my shoulder and smiled as best he could. "Dr. Sanders asked us to leave Bo with him until tomorrow. They're going to observe him and see if he'll…"

"Live?" I finished his sentence as tears spilled down my cheeks. I ran into my mother's embrace, and we sobbed together.

Bo was more than a pet—he was a cherished member of our family. Throughout that long day, Mother phoned the vet's office for updates. Bo was alive, but not better. Time stood still, and despair descended like a shroud.

On the one hand, I could not wait until tomorrow to find out if he had lived through the night…on the other hand, I didn't want to face tomorrow if he hadn't. In the meantime, I prayed.

I ran into my mother's embrace, and we sobbed together. Bo was more than a pet—he was a cherished member of our family.

~Karen Jurgens

I awoke early the next day and braced for the worst. As we convened around the breakfast table, I held my breath. "Any news?"

Before Mother could respond, the phone rang. She answered and indicated to us it was the vet's office calling. I continued to hold my breath and prayed for good news.

Mother listened quietly for several minutes. Finally, she hung up the receiver and turned to us with a sigh of relief. "Bo made it!"

Dad and I cheered, but Mother's serious expression stopped us. "Dr. Sanders said two employees sat up with him all night. The poor little thing paced around the office, struggling to breathe. They think Bo has developed allergies to the Arizona desert." She paused, "Unfortunately, there's nothing more they can do for him. Dr. Sanders is asking us to take him home."

Overjoyed at first, I clapped my hands in ecstasy before I realized *the rest of the story...* then froze. "But if there's nothing else they can do, that means...he's coming home *to die*?" My throat constricted.

At that morbid thought, my parents probably felt as sick as I did. But for now, bringing Bo home, even to die, was most important.

His homecoming was bittersweet. Although still sick and wheezing, he was visibly relieved to be in familiar surroundings and with family. We tried to make him as comfortable as possible with his favorite toys on soft blankets in the kitchen where we could keep a close eye.

By nightfall, Bo's condition had worsened. Exhausted, my mother and I each headed to bed, but my father chose to stay in the kitchen with him all night. Since Bo usually slept on my parent's bed, my dad made a pallet to lie next to him so Bo wouldn't be afraid. Listening to his loud wheezing upset us, but no one voiced what we all believed—Bo wouldn't make it through a second night.

I climbed into bed with a heavy heart, pleading with the Lord for Bo's life. A dampened pillow and a pile of wet tissues later, I did the hardest thing I have ever done. I surrendered Bo to God. But just as I stopped crying and drifted into twilight sleep, I heard a gentle voice speak softly inside my spirit.

The dog will be alright.

My eyelids popped open, and I was instantly awake. The voice had resonated inside me, loud and clear. I had heard older relatives relate stories about hearing God's voice, and I also recalled the Bible story of Samuel, "Now the Lord came and stood and called as at other times, "Samuel! Samuel!" And Samuel answered, "Speak, for

Your servant hears" (1 Samuel 3:10 NKJV). Total amazement swept over me at what I had just experienced. If that were God's voice, Bo *would* live. I praised God for His reassurance and promise of healing. Sadness fled, and new-found hope rocked me to sleep.

When I awoke early the next morning, the house was quiet. Not knowing if that was a good sign or not, I hurried to the kitchen, my heart pounding. I clung to God's promise that the dog would be alive.

"How is he?"

My parents turned and smiled. They stepped back so I could see our beloved pet, eating from his bowl like his old self. It was a miracle! Yes, God's promise had come true.

When Bo saw me, he stopped eating and came to greet me,- all wiggles and licks. His asthma had all but disappeared. In fact, he continued in good health for ten more years, asthma-free.

That experience boosted my faith up several notches, and I learned to trust God in a new way. I realized He must love us very deeply to console us when we grieve for a sick pet. I knew for certain that the dog's healing had come from God's hand and not from a veterinarian's. Most importantly, I now know the answer to my question. God loves and cares for all His creation—and He is willing to heal our family pets.

Have you witnessed God's healing for a family pet?

Thank you, Jesus, for Your loving mercy toward us. You demonstrate Your tender compassion when You heal our sick pets as readily as You do our human family members.

Amen.

A Godly Heritage

Karen Jurgens

Train up a child in the way he should go,
And when he is old he will not depart from it.

~Proverbs 22:6 NKJV

As a child, learning about God and witnessing my family live out their faith was an ordinary part of life. Sixty years ago, it was a different world. But one thing that never changes is God's Word.

My godly heritage is rooted in the influence of my maternal great-grandparents. Their Kentucky farm was a long three-hours' drive from Cincinnati.

As a child plagued by motion sickness, I always dreaded the last leg of that trip. We might as well have been driving on the back of a curvy snake.

When smooth highway had changed into winding, narrow dirt roads covered in gravel, I peered out the back window to watch our car's wake boil behind us. I prayed for the interminable swaying to end as the car's wheels slowly crunched around sharp turns. After what seemed like forever, we rounded a final bend, and the white farmhouse jumped out with its white pillars and airy porch extending welcoming arms.

Pure relief flooded through me as I exited the back seat and inhaled fresh country air, which helped settle my stomach.

Halfway to the front entrance we were greeted by my great-aunt Rosie—a schoolteacher who had never married—followed by my great-grandparents. I felt swallowed up in bear hugs and kisses as they escorted us to the porch to get settled on swings and rocking chairs. Conversation and laughter buzzed all around me. Unconditional love and warm hospitality swirled, anchoring me securely in my family's love.

...love one another fervently with a pure heart...

~1 Peter 1:22b NKJV

The highlight of the welcoming company meant sitting at Grandma's dinner table, and I anticipated the usual feast, fresh from their garden and animal stock.

Fresh churned butter with homemade jams and honey stood ready for topping hot biscuits and cornbread.

Aunt Rosie poured out glasses of cold milk produced from their dairy cows. Platters of fried chicken and bowls of vegetables hot off the stove wafted under our noses.

We took our seats and spread napkins on our laps, then bowed our heads as Grandpa offered a long prayer of thanks. After we had passed the food and everyone had piled their plates high, I digested the adult conversation that was as wholesome as the organic food.

About midway through the meal, talk would usually turn to questions about God's Word, and Grandpa would patiently answer from his well of godly wisdom. Those precious seeds of godliness were planted in my soul at an early age.

'But other seed fell on good ground and yielded a crop that sprang up, increased and produced: some thirtyfold, some sixty, and some a hundred.'

~Mark 4:8 NKJV

After dinner, the adults rocked on the front porch to visit and enjoy the sunset. I played with their dog, Pal, or tried to catch one of the wild kittens who lived under the house. As the dusk of evening rose, I chased fireflies that dotted the air with their diamond-brilliance. Sometimes I even caught one and watched its flashing light between my fingers.

When I tired of my games, I, too, would rock and listen to Aunt Rosie discuss who-married-whom—eleven children and their descendants spanning three generations were challenging to track. That was how they passed down our family tree's lineage in those days, albeit orally and memorized.

By the time the trees blended into darkness and the volume of chirping crickets and hooting owls turned high, everyone retreated into the house—but not to retire to bed. My mother always brought a gift of fruits, cheeses, crackers, and candy for sharing late at night. We congregated in the living room in our robes and slippers to share a late night's snack along with more conversation.

Oh, taste and see that the Lord is good; Blessed is the man who trusts in Him!

~Psalm 34:8 NKJV

However, no one said goodnight until after evening prayers. First, Grandpa would read verses from his huge, thick Bible, and the adults would discuss their meaning. Often, they would tell stories of testimonies they had heard, such as missionaries in foreign lands who had experienced miracles.

Sometimes Grandpa would tell about his vision where he had witnessed Saul's conversion on the road to Damascus—a vision so real, he insisted it had really happened (Grandma would shake her head to the others and smile).

One fascinating story involved my Aunt Bessie as a child who had seen a vision of Jesus one night when she was walking to the outhouse.

Another one—my favorite—was about my mother when she was a little girl and had spent the night with two missionaries staying in a cabin across the road. In the middle of the night, one of my great-aunts happened to look out a front window and saw the roof of the cabin burning with orange-red flames. She screamed and woke up the entire household. The men pulled on their pants and ran to rescue them, only to discover that there had not been a fire at all. People always said that the Shekinah glory of God had manifested on the roof after their long prayer meeting that night.

'Surely the Lord our God has shown us His glory and His greatness,
and we have heard His voice from the midst of the fire.'

~Deuteronomy 5:24a NKJV

After our discussion we would all kneel, facing our chairs, and each person would take a turn to pray aloud. I especially remember Grandpa praying for all his family—*all of his seed*—and asking God for His salvation and blessings to rest on each one.

I would often fall asleep to the lull of those sweet prayers ascending to heaven, sensing the presence of listening angels who gently wafted peace through the house with their feathered wings.

Rejoice always, pray without ceasing, in everything give thanks; for
this is the will of God in Christ Jesus for you.

~1 Thessalonians 5:16-18 NKJV

The most precious realization of my godly heritage has been experiencing those prayers as my life's bedrock. Grandpa's words still ring in my memory, and I know I am walking across long corridors of prayer laid by him and generations of godly family before him. The knowledge of how God has worked in my life through this foundation of prayer underscores the importance of its continuance. I, too, am laying another layer of prayer on top of my forefathers' as a path for my future generations to trod.

Grandpa's words still ring in my memory, and I know I am walking across long corridors of prayer laid by him and generations of godly family before him.

~Karen Jurgens

How important is it to establish godly ancestral roots?

Supremely.

Regardless of possessing a long line of godly ancestry or being the first generation to establish those roots—*pray.* Pray for your future generations—for salvation, blessings, and godly lives—so they may add another layer of prayer for their future generations to cross.

Are you praying a godly heritage for your future generations?

Dear Lord, thank You for Your salvation and for generations of godly families. May we also pray a corridor of prayer to bless our future generations.

In Jesus's Name, Amen.

Comforted to Comfort

Julie Souza Bradley Lilly

I was a widow at fifty-three. My precious first husband, Jim, developed cancer and died before he could see his sixtieth birthday.

In the days and weeks surrounding his passing, the Lord sent several people to minister to me. All of their kindnesses were of comfort, but it was the voices of other widows, my sisters in Christ, that spoke with greatest volume.

Knowing they had suffered similar grief and loss elevated their voices above others. They had survived what to me felt unsurvivable. I looked to them as a roadmap, as I searched for hope and a way of escape from the unending heartache.

It was the voices of other widows, my sisters in Christ, that spoke with greatest volume. Knowing they had suffered similar grief and loss elevated their voices above others.

~Julie Souza Bradley Lilly

Successfully navigating the waters of great difficulty gives us a voice to those who similarly suffer. Experience carries more weight than mere information ever could.

We are never alone in our suffering. The Father intimately knows our grief. Through Jesus Christ, He knows our pain, disappointment and betrayal. And it is with great compassion that He longs to comfort us. 2 Corinthians 1:3-5 NIV reads, "Praise be to the God and Father of our Lord Jesus Christ, the Father of compassion and the God of all comfort, who comforts us in all our troubles, so that we can comfort those in any trouble with the comfort we ourselves receive from God. For just as we share abundantly in the sufferings of Christ, so also our comfort abounds through Christ."

Cling to Him in your suffering, beloved. Listen intently for His comforting words. They come not from judgment, but compassion and love. He comes to the aid of widows. He is the Father to the fatherless. He is the mender of shattered families and the healer of broken hearts and bodies. He offers hope when all feels hopeless, and an unexpected doorway to joy in our mourning. God comforts us in Luke with these words, "The Spirit of the LORD is upon Me [Jesus Christ], because He has anointed Me to … heal the brokenhearted" (Luke 4:18b).

Press into Him, seek Him, and somewhere along the way you will also find your voice of comfort to help others who hurt. Our brokenness and pain transform into strength and influence when we invite His strength into our weakness. Our test becomes our testimony and our grief a doorway to joy.

Have you grappled with grief and emerged stronger? Share your experience.

Heavenly Father, hold me as Your child, for I am broken by grief. As You hold me, fill me to overflowing with Your peace. As I am being filled, help me to lavishly pour out upon others from your abundance of comfort that You comfort me with. Help me to share the joy I have gained by being in Your presence.

In Jesus's Name, Amen.

Repeating Life in a Dream

Lee Ann Mancini

I look forward to putting on my pajamas, reading a good book, and laying my head on my pillow at the end of a busy day. I also enjoy taking a nap during the day if time and circumstance permit.

Brian Halligan, the CEO of an eight-billion-dollar company, takes a nap every day during working hours. In fact, he converted a room in his company's office into a "nap area" for his workers.

In Proverbs, we read, "When you lie down, you will not be afraid; when you lie down, your sleep will be sweet" (Proverbs 3:24 NIV).

As much as I enjoy sleeping, what I really love is having pleasant dreams. The night before my son's twenty-ninth birthday, I had the best dream of my life. It made me so happy, I woke up with tears streaming down my face.

In my dream, my daughter and son ran to me and jumped onto my lap. I could feel their little arms and hands wrapped around me, and I could see their tiny, innocent faces. I heard my son exclaim in his six-year-old voice, "Mommy, I am so happy! Today is my birthday!" I replied, "Yes, son, it is, and we are going to have the best birthday party for you!"

When I awoke, I thanked the Lord for allowing me to revisit this precious moment in time with my children, recalling that I should always rejoice.

This reminds me of a verse in 1 Thessalonians. Paul writes, "Rejoice always, pray continually, give thanks in all circumstances; for this is God's will for you in Christ Jesus" (1 Thessalonians 5:16-18 NIV).

When my son came over to celebrate his birthday, I embraced him a little longer than I usually do.

Puzzled, he asked, "Mom, are you okay?"

I told him, "Yes, I just missed you! Happy birthday, son!"

Shortly afterwards, I had a conversation with my niece, who is pregnant with her first child. She was having a hard time deciding whether to return to work or be a stay-at-home mom.

I showed her my favorite portrait of my children when they were four and six, saying, "These are my babies. Do you know where they went? I haven't seen them for many years. I miss them terribly." I told her I would give anything to hold them in my arms one more time, and then I told her about my dream.

Sleep is beneficial to our health in more ways that we can imagine. So is resting in the Lord, and we find many Bible verses that assure us of His care for us. But there is something else I want you to notice; God is Father.

We are God's children, deeply loved and cared for ... by the God who framed the Universe.

~Lee Ann Mancini

Just as my son and daughter are precious to me, as I am sure your children are to you, we are God's children, deeply loved and cared for meticulously by the God who framed the Universe. He adopts us into His family as soon as we trust Jesus Christ as our personal Savior.

Think about the majesty of a Father who would redeem us from our sins by the blood atonement of His only begotten Son. That's love. And Jesus willingly paid redemption's price, going to Calvary's cross of His own accord.

God rejoices in our decision, saying to His redeemed sons and daughters that they can call Him "Daddy."

In Galatians, Paul writes, "But when the fullness of the time had come, God sent forth His Son, born of a woman, born under the law, to redeem those who were under the law, that we might receive the adoption as sons. And because you are sons, God has sent forth the Spirit of His Son into your hearts, crying out, 'Abba, Father!'" (Galatians 4:4-6 NKJV).

This is a truth that is even more restful than physical sleep, that I can call on the God of the Universe, rest in His care, call Him "Daddy," and be forgiven of my transgressions.

Now that's a dream world I want to live in and stay awake while I ponder the vastness of His love.

How does knowing God as Father bring you a peace that is better than the best dream?

Heavenly Father, thank You for You allowing me to revisit my past and see Your guiding hand and forgiving manner, as I also look toward the future. My hope remains steadfast in You! Thank You that as my Heavenly Father, You set a course for my life, and You bring me peace that is more restful than sleep.

In Jesus's Name, Amen.

The Family that Fights

Shanda Neighbors

God resists the proud, but gives grace to the humble.

~James 4:6b NKJV

"I'm running away."

"Great! Where are we going?" My husband clearly missed the point.

(Sigh.)

"I'm running away from *you* too," he added, his lip turning upwards at the corner. He needed to know marriage and parenting had equal shares in driving me nuts.

"Oh, okay. I will stay. I'll be quiet."

The wedding vows sometimes feel somber. "Till death" it is, but sometimes I genuinely want to get away from them. The space I converted to an office offers no solitude. They always find me. Even when they don't physically intrude, their banshee and hyena noises do.

The last hunt for isolation led me to our family car, parked behind closed garage doors. I outfitted my new retreat with water, snacks, my computer, and a Bible. Still, even from the garage, I could hear them cackling at the kitchen table. Apparently, rough housing and chase games are our family values. These compete fiercely with my writing process. Additionally, my folks ask me a zillion questions and for my help locating a litany of things. I've put real thought into listing "professional finder" as a job skill on my resumé.

It's not just that they annoy me, but also that we don't always get along. At times we are downright mean to each other. Perhaps it's just my family. Admittedly, we're an odd bunch. Or perhaps it's lots of families, and I'm just being more honest than socially acceptable.

Pause for the truth. The things we argue about are so trivial, I wonder if the conversations we have are actually happening.

"Is it a hot dog, or a hot dog sandwich?"

"Is boxed stuffing and cranberry sauce better than homemade?"

My husband says the wrong things, which means I get to work on my temper. Our teenager can be moody, which forces me to be a spiritually mature parent—a position I don't always welcome. Our nine-year-old is really sensitive. That doesn't fit with me, since my natural contribution to this dysfunctional mix consists of cutting words mixed with sarcasm.

While it's true my family fights, by the strength of the Lord, we also fight for each other.

~Shanda Neighbors

Still, God put us together.

While it's true my family fights, by the strength of the Lord, we also fight for each other. My loved ones have demonstrated extreme patience toward me, along with grace, humility, and forgiveness. We forget wrongs more quickly and say "I'm sorry" often. Sometimes we speak those words because we feel them, but more often it's because we know it's what our Heavenly Father wants.

Humility to His perfection holds us together.

We lean on His understanding. A round won by the enemy doesn't determine the entire battle, nor does it change the plans and purposes of God for us.

God says in His Word, "The wisdom that is from above is first pure, then peaceable, gentle, willing to yield, full of mercy and good fruits, without partiality and without hypocrisy" (James 3:17b-4:1 NKJV). This Scripture offers God's wisdom for disputes. He counsels me to be pure, peaceable, and gentle. He tells me to yield my right and to offer good fruits of mercy. When I am sincere in following His guidance, I can be the wife, mother, and person I desire to be.

Despite our ups and downs, my family's favorite place to be is together. Talking about biblical things, dreams, politics, or sometimes not talking at all. We laugh a lot, and we're way more immature than we need to be. We fellowship around food too often, and we are the laziest bunch of folks on Sundays. We are as opposite as any group of people can be, but we love each other. God continues to teach us that, and sometimes He uses our conflicts and sins to do so. We are not perfect or special. But we are surrendered.

It's easy to love a perfect family. But what do we do when our reality falls short, and we are sloppy versions of perfection? We resist the urge to judge or fix them so we feel like a success. We let go of the scenario we envisioned and allow our people to be a flawed work in progress while we work on ourselves, learning to hear His still, small whispers of correction.

Even as I say these things with conviction, I realize not all issues are the same. Some require counselling. If these conflicts are factors within your family dynamics, take heart. God has given you amazing abilities to grow in Him. Remain humble before Him. Ask His correction and direction. Nothing is impossible with God, and He is an expert at restoring families. Take it from a woman who has considered divorcing her husband and teenagers—it does get better.

What is a godly trait you can model that will demonstrate love for your family?

Heavenly Father, Thank You for my family. Help me to humble myself so You can guide me in my treatment of my family. Correct me where I am wrong and lead me in Your wisdom. Help me to walk in Your love toward every family member.

In Jesus's Name, Amen.

"Daddy's Girl"

Stephanie Pavlantos

God is not ashamed to be called their God.

~Hebrews 11:16b NKJV

Dad was fifty years old when I was born, and I was a "daddy's girl."

Daddy held me on his lap when the doctor gave my vaccines with a gun-like device that left a scar the size of a dime on my upper arm. He taught me to ride my bike. He brought me and my siblings homemade donuts before leaving for work. He had plans to buy a big farm.

But circumstances changed that collapsed that dream...

After my sixth birthday, Dad suffered a massive stroke, which left him paralyzed on his right side. Because of this event, even at six-years-old, I knew my life would be different. Everything seemed to change.

Dad's personality and body were different—and he felt broken. He was unable to do most of the things he used to do. My mom and my five sisters did all the work.

My dad would sit on the porch watching us cut the grass, fearing we would get hurt. When we complained, he would say, "I know, I wish I could do it."

I now understand how much it hurt him to watch his daughters do "his" work.

At first, he struggled with feelings of uselessness, which led to severe depression that he overcame.

Dad may not have been able to achieve the physical and financial dreams he desired, but his faith became stronger because of these difficulties, so much that his unapologetic faith became his gift to us.

Faith framed Dad's life.

He prayed for us constantly. My dad prayed for strength and comfort for Mom, who, by default, had to work long hours to support the family. Dad prayed for each of us girls to know God as he did. He valued our salvation most. Every day, he read the Bible to us at dinner, and at bedtime he prayed over us, placing his hand on our heads as we knelt by his easy chair.

Dad may not have been able to achieve the physical and financial dreams he desired, but his faith became stronger because of these difficulties, so much that this unapologetic faith became his gift to us.

~Stephanie Pavlantos

My dad may have felt useless in his body, but his spirit was full of life that comes from the Son of God. He did not realize the influence he had on his six daughters.

Even from his wheelchair, he spoke life over us and planted seeds for an eternal purpose. We may never know on this side of heaven the impact we have on others—but God does. He died one month after I married, and I am thankful God allowed him to "walk" me down the aisle.

In Hebrews 11, the author shares how the faith of many Old Testament saints influenced those around them. Like my father, these men and women were righteous in God's sight because of their great faith and obedience in times of trials and persecution.

They suffered mocking, persecution, and imprisonment, yet their faith remained steadfast. Hebrews 11:38 states that they were people, "of whom the world was not worthy." They lived and died for their God.

Hebrews 11:13 ESV reads, "These all died in faith, not receiving the things promised, but having seen them and greeted them from afar, and having acknowledged that they were strangers and exiles on the earth."

A few verses later, the author writes, "Therefore God is not ashamed to be called their God" (Hebrews 11:16b NKJV). This verse is in the present tense. Why? It is because God was not ashamed then, and He is unashamed now to be their God.

Friend, God is not ashamed to be your God, either.

No matter how we see ourselves—as useless in our jobs or as a stay-at-home mom, or how many times we have messed up and felt as though we have let God and others down—if you belong to God, He is not ashamed of you, and He receives you as His child.

If you do not have someone who models immovable faith in your family, then be that person to a family member. Your eternal reward is priceless.

Who do you know who, despite challenges, serves God faithfully.

Heavenly Father, Thank You that You are not ashamed to be my God. Thank You for being a loving Father and for giving Your Son, Jesus Christ, to give me life. I am Yours for eternity.

In Jesus's Name, Amen.

A Godly Influence

Glenda Shouse

You shall teach them to your children.

~Deuteronomy 11:19 NKJV

One of my fondest childhood memories was hearing my grandmother pray every night.

In our small house, my sister and I shared a room with Grandmother. We would fall asleep as she steadfastly prayed to God, never missing a single night. We could tell she loved the one to whom she prayed.

The sound of Grandmother talking to the Lord was comforting, and I will never forget those blessed moments. She was a wonderful woman who had a godly influence in our lives.

Grandmother's faith influenced me to accept Jesus Christ as my personal Savior. Because I witnessed the genuine relationship Grandmother had with Him, I desired to follow her example.

Paul reminds Timothy of the godly influences his grandmother and mother had on his faith as he writes, "When I call to remembrance the genuine faith that is in you, which dwelt first in your grandmother, Lois and your mother Eunice, and I am persuaded is in you also" (2 Timothy 1:5a NKJV).

What a wonderful heritage it is for us to live out our faith in Jesus Christ before our children and grandchildren, just as my grandmother did for me and my sister.

Our actions can be more meaningful than what we say. Sometimes it is the small things we do that make a lasting impression on our children and those around us, like thanking God for our meal, reading our Bible, or praying for others. These are straightforward ways we can honor and glorify God as we go about our day.

The sound of Grandmother talking to the Lord was comforting, and I will never forgot those blessed moments.

~Glenda Shouse

Even though Grandmother was a wonderful witness to me, I still had to respond to God's calling upon my life and accept the gift of salvation through Jesus Christ. I finally understood Jesus had already done everything for me and all I had to do was pray, "Lord Jesus, thank You for dying on the cross for me, forgive me of my sins. Come into my heart and be my Lord and Savior." This is the best decision I've ever made. The Gospel is simple, but sometimes it takes time for the Holy Spirit to prepare our hearts to receive Jesus and surrender to His wooing.

Friend, once you receive the gift of salvation, be sure to share your newfound faith with others. If you are already saved, be confident by sharing. Our children, family, and friends are watching, and they may model your faith because you took time to show them your love for Christ Jesus and for them.

Who is someone who has influenced your faith in Jesus Christ?

Heavenly Father, thank You for the opportunities You provide for us to share our faith. Help us to always be prepared to do so.

In Jesus's Name, Amen.

My Adoption

Sandra Stein

We love because he first loved us.

~1 John 4:19 NIV

I grew up with a family, but I didn't grow up in a family.

The term, "family" had little meaning to me. Yes, there was a man, a woman, and children in the house, and I may have called them "Mom" and "Dad," but our family wasn't what it was supposed to be.

A family has love in it.

My family had the opposite of love—violence, abuse, and hatred.

My heart-ached to be in a loving family. Secretly, I wanted to be adopted into my parent's friend's family because of the love I saw them give their children. I took notice at a young age of how other families lived, communicated, and interacted. It was obvious my family lacked the caring, nurturing, and bonding I witnessed other families sharing.

It wasn't until I became an adult that I found out I had been adopted. How so? My adoption notice came from the Bible.

In Ephesians, we read, "God decided in advance to adopt us into his own family by bringing us to himself through Jesus Christ. This is what he wanted to do, and it gave him great pleasure" (Ephesians 1:5 NLT).

With my newfound adoption, I experienced true love—the kind only my Heavenly Father can give. With my newfound realization that Father God loved me, I in turn could love others.

Today, I have a family of my own where the love of God abounds in measures far beyond what I thought I could realize as a child growing up in an abusive home.

Those days are over and gone, and I have learned godly values by reading my Bible. The Bible is the guidance I use to gain the knowledge to raise my children in security, acceptance, morals, and most of all—love.

It wasn't until I became an adult that I found out I had been adopted. How so? My adoption notice came from the Bible.

~Sandra Stein

I find great comfort in a Bible verse from Romans. Paul writes, "For you did not receive the spirit of bondage again to fear, but you received the Spirit of adoption by which we cry out, "Abba, Father" (Romans 8:15 NKJV).

I may have grown up in bondage and abuse, but those days are over and gone. Now, I see myself as adopted by the Best of the best--for truly I am God's child. I call God "Abba," which is an endearing New Testament (Aramaic) term used for "Father." He loves me even more than the loving family I secretly wanted to be adopted into. I am grateful He showed me this truth.

It is the same for you, friend. No matter what situation you grew up in, and no matter whether you have grown up in an abusive family, or a loving family, you have a Heavenly Father who loves you and adopts you as His own child. Permit Him to show you the depths, height, and width of His abundant love for you.

Even before I met God, He loved me, and He loves you as much as He loves me. To God, each of us is His favorite child. His love is vast, for only the most loving god would sacrifice his son. Father God loved us so much that He sent His only begotten Son, Jesus Christ, to die on the cross, rise from the dead, and ascend into heaven to prepare a heavenly home for us so that we can live eternally in His love.

Father God hears the cries of His children, as He heard mine. He is here for you right now. Call upon Him, and ask Him to reveal to you how much He loves you.

God. Loves YOU.

Share your adoption story by God. If you are not yet saved, call upon Him today, to adopt you as His own. His arms are open wide, and He is ready to receive you.

Heavenly Father, thank You for blessing me, and for bringing me into Your own spiritual family. I forgive all those who have wronged me, including family members. Thank You for the love You show me every day. I am blessed to know I am Your child whom You dearly love.

In Jesus's Name, Amen.

Dancing Shoes

Diane Virginia

For God so loved the world, that he gave his only begotten Son, that whosoever believeth in him should not perish, but have everlasting life.

~John 3:16 KJV

I have become a collector of hearts, but I do not collect just any hearts. They are gifts from my daughter, Danielle. Each is like a time capsule, capturing a memory from her youth.

One is a foil heart of two colors.

Yet another is a heart-shaped rock she found in the garden. On that day, she skipped to me, squealing with delight, carrying her little rock. We washed it under the hose, and she cradled it. Then, she kissed me on the cheek, told me her little treasure belonged to me, and ran off to play. Periodically she would check to make sure I was cradling the heart to her satisfaction.

One heart is of twisted wire, fashioned as a pendant for me to wear.

 Another is of clay. Because she was older, it is detailed and thinner, with the letters "I" and "U" flanking this heart.

I look at these hearts often, as I remember that my daughter will forever be in my heart as I am in hers.

What do Danielle's hearts have to do with dancing shoes? Let me tell you a story that will give you the answer. I invite you to enter the world of make-believe and simple truths....

Pretend you're a little girl aged four-and-a-half. Yes, "and-a-half" is important when you are that age.

At this time, you are learning to love Jesus.

You love to run, bounce on couches, and play bowling with Daddy where you and your brother get to be the pins, and a giant beach ball is the bowling ball. Yes, you're an active girl.

Your hair is golden with hints of red, and your locks are shoulder length.

You are taking dancing classes. You learn to pirouette, point your toes, jump, and twirl. The teacher whom you are learning from loves Jesus.

Then it happens...

You are in church with Daddy, Mommy, and your little brother. A holy hush comes upon the Sunday congregation. There's a stirring as spontaneous worship begins.

You listen in...

A gentleman starts singing in the balcony. He is joined by a lady in the choir. Another lady in the nave begins to sing. The congregation joins in. Soon, the worship becomes exuberant.

You tug at Momma's hem, "Momma, can I dance?"

"What, sweetheart?"

"Jesus is here. Can I dance?"

"You may."

With permission granted, you run the aisle of the church, twirling in exuberant worship. Your dance is the perfect picture of what Jesus says about the innocent trust of a child, "Let the children come to me; do not hinder them, for to such belongs the kingdom of God" (Mark 10:14b ESV).

To your parents' delight, you worship as only a child can fully do. You are carefree, real, trusting, and innocent. The joy you display comes from within your heart. You make Mommy and Daddy proud that day, and we smile really big. All day.

The next morning, you point to the heart-cross pendant your momma has worn for your whole life. You tell me, "I wanna wear a cross with a heart just like you."

"Sweetheart," I say, "when you know what it means to be saved, Momma promises you, I'll get you a heart-cross pendant."

You pout.

"It's just that... well, sweetie, you're four."

"And-a-half."

"Your birthday is real soon. We'll celebrate it."

"I wanna wear a heart. With a cross." You cross your arms and swing a foot.

"When you understand what it means to be saved...."

"But Mommy, I do understand."

"Well then, how about you tell Mommy what you believe about Jesus."

"My Jesus died on the cross, and He's alive."

"True...."

"And He loves me this much!" You spread your hands as wide as you can.

"That's true too."

"And when I put my dancing shoes on, I can feel Him right heeeeeere...." You point to your heart and twirl.

"I will get you a heart with a cross." I say, "because I see that you do understand."

Sometimes the inner heart puts on dancing shoes. And sometimes the one who believes is a little girl, aged four-and-a-half, who knows without reservation that John 3:16 is real.

~Diane Virginia

I'd love to say I bought my daughter Danielle that first heart-cross pendant, but I did not. You see, Danielle's dance teacher came to me that next Sunday and she told me how much my four-and-a-half year-old was really into worship. My daughter's teacher was impressed not by the perfection of my child's moves, but by the spirit in which she performed them.

She asked permission to give Danielle a gift. I agreed. She handed Danielle a tiny box.

Inside was a pendant—a cross within a sparkly heart.

Danielle jumped for joy! But I cried, knowing the Lord Himself had confirmed to me she really did know what it meant to be saved.

The Bible says, "For with the heart man believeth" (Romans 10:10a KJV). May I add, that sometimes the inner heart puts on dancing shoes. And sometimes the one who believes is a little girl, aged four-and-a-half, who knows without reservation that John 3:16 is real.

Share a memory of childlike faith you've witnessed or experienced.

Heavenly Father, I ask You to give me childlike faith, in all of its innocence, so I can worshipYou in reckless abandon.

In Jesus Christ's Name, Amen.

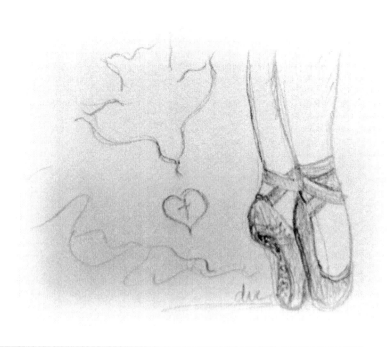

Incredible Journeys

Evelyn Wells

Fear not, for I am with you; Be not dismayed, for I am your God. I will strengthen you, Yes, I will help you, I will uphold you with My righteous right hand.

~Isaiah 41:10 NKJV

I held Clancy close, my heart breaking.

As Dr. Martha hugged me, I saw tears in her eyes. Experiencing her compassion that day gave me the strength God had promised in Isaiah 41:10. I knew I would grieve and miss Clancy terribly, but I also knew God would strengthen us and He would receive Clancy.

My journey with Clancy had come to an end after fourteen years.

Because of the outstanding veterinary care Dr. Martha provided, Clancy had been able to enjoy a much longer life than he otherwise would have had.

Clancy had come into my life by default. Being aware of my love for cats, my niece, Carol, had called me. Matter of fact, as always, she said, "I have a Siamese kitten for you. He's six weeks old. When can you pick him up? Or would you like me to bring him to you?"

Every good thing given and every perfect gift is from above, coming down from the Father of lights, with whom there is no variation or shifting shadow.

~James 1:17 NASB

My journey with Clancy began the moment Carol placed this tiny, Lilac-Point Siamese kitten into my outstretched hands. He was a family member to me. He was the four-footed variety but loved as much as any of us.

Clancy loved being in our big yard and enjoyed patrolling the area just inside the tree line. He took his responsibilities seriously as "watch cat." He chased away dogs and other cats who ventured into his yard.

Deer passed through often and sometimes stopped to graze. Clancy liked them—one time I saw him approach a doe and stand on his hind legs to touch noses with her.

Clancy was a loving kitty and spent his evenings contentedly purring himself to sleep in my lap as I relaxed in my easy chair. He spent the night curled up beside me on my bed and belied the myth that felines are indifferent to their humans.

My sister lived next door. Clancy believed he had two moms and visited her every day where he often curled up on her bed for a nap. When I was gone overnight, Clancy stayed with his "Aunt Jean."

My house felt empty that first evening, and after hours of tears and loneliness, I realized the most fitting tribute to Clancy would be to adopt another cat.

~Evelyn Wells

My house felt empty that first evening after Clancy's homegoing, and I cried for hours. I felt very lonely too. Finally, I realized the most fitting tribute to Clancy would be to adopt another cat.

Then the Lord God said, "It is not good for the man to be alone; I will make him a helper suitable for him." Out of the ground the Lord God formed every beast of the field and every bird of the sky, and brought them to the man to see what he would call them; and whatever the man called a living creature, that was its name.

~Genesis 2:18-19 NASB

Wavering between guilt and resolve, I went online to find a cat most in need of a home.

I checked animal shelters, veterinary clinics, and humane societies. I must have read the descriptions of a hundred homeless cats before I found my new kitty under a listing of Calicos.

The picture on the computer screen showed a small adult cat with soft gray fur. She had an off-white underside and paws, with a peachy color brushed here and there.

Her face looked unnaturally thin, and her ears seemed enormous. Her picture showed evidence of a difficult life, but instead of defeat and resignation, the expression in her eyes was one of expectancy and hope.

The animal rescue had discovered her patiently waiting beside a box containing her kittens. I was drawn to her, knowing her kittens would not be hard to place, but the chances of this momma kitty finding a home was slim-to-none. She was at the point of starvation, and she had dull, thinning hair, with every rib was visible.

In his hand is the life of every creature and the breath of all mankind.

~Job 12:10 NIV

I named my new kitty Bella.

While Bella can never take Clancy's place, this now healthy and beautiful cat has established a place of her own. Thus, an incredible journey with my new friend Bella has begun, and I am loving every minute of it.

I praise God He befriends us with four-footed family members.

God loves to give us good gifts. Reflect on special family members He has given you, including your pets.

Thank You, Heavenly Father for Your presence in all of my journeys. Thank You that You provide creatures for us to love as deeply as we love our human family members.

In Jesus's Name, Amen.

Who's Telling Whom?

Martin Wiles

Repeat them again and again to your children. Talk about them when you are at home and when you are on the road, when you are going to bed and when you are getting up.

~Deuteronomy 6:7 NLT

I listened to the stories for hours.

I don't know whether I was an abnormal kid or not, but I loved to sit with my grandparents and listen to them tell stories. My granddaddy's favorite was how he had to quit school when he was in the sixth grade. His father had died from cancer, and someone had to run the family farm. As the oldest boy still living at home, the job fell to him.

My grandmother kept the family connections straight for me. She reminded me of which kids went with which parents, how so-and-so was connected to the family, and what their current situation in life was. Since she was the family matriarch, relatives called her to catch her up on the family news.

But things have changed.

All my grandparents have passed on. My daddy and momma didn't know or share as many of the family stories, so I had no one to ask once my grandparents died. Then my father died, and my mother began to have memory issues. She can no longer keep the details straight.

Sharing the stories has now fallen to me, and it makes me feel old, even though I'm only sixty.

The trouble is that no one asks to hear the stories. My children are young adults, but only interested in the busyness of their own lives. My brothers are nine and ten years younger than I am, and even they rarely ask to hear the family stories. Many of the family stories, my siblings and children don't even know. And my grandchildren don't even know there are stories.

As time passes, my family stories seem to fade from everyone's memory. God didn't want that to happen with another important family story—the one that told of the commands He had given His followers.

He wanted parents and grandparents to repeat these guidelines...commands...to their children and grandchildren. Otherwise, they would forget, and forgetting would impact their culture and society.

Sharing the stories has now fallen to me... The trouble is that no one asks to hear the stories.

~Martin Wiles

God hasn't changed His guidelines. Neither has He changed His expectations of us to share them with my family, friends, and acquaintances. When we do, the world becomes a better place because God's principles lead to clean living and a pure society—at all levels. People will love more, show more kindness, and treat others with respect. But if we quit telling the story, the opposite will happen.

Make time to share God's story with others—especially your family—and make the world a better place.

Heavenly Father, thank You for entrusting me to tell the stories of my family. Most of all, thank You that the greatest story I can share with my family is the salvation message found exclusively in Jesus Christ my Lord. Help me to tell of Him often.

In Jesus's Name, Amen.

Friendships

Friends

Martin Wiles

You walked into my life—
An angel of mercy,
A guardian of light
For a darkened soul.

You took my hand
And led me into joy.
You lifted my heart
To an enduring height.

The plain upon which we walk
Is not lightly traversed—
Only few find its treasure,
But we travel undaunted.

Now we two are one,
Entwined in mangled cords,
A bond formed with love
That time cannot concede.

As the wind is free,
But bound among the twines,
So, our spirits are free,
Yet fixed in friendship's web.

A Letter to God

Ed Chappelle

Have I not commanded you? Be strong and courageous. Do not be frightened, and do not be dismayed, for the Lord your God is with you wherever you go."

~Joshua 1:9 ESV

Dear God,

Remember the time when I was five years old, and I almost got hit by a car, but the car stopped in time, and all I received was a blow to my stomach? You were there with me.

How about the time I was hit in the head by a baseball while playing Little League Baseball? You were there, and You helped me to heal.

Then there was the time Mom made a birthday cake, but the family dog ate it. That was funny, even though Mom didn't think so. I felt You did, though. You shared many of my fun adventures, and I imagine You laughed with me.

God, then there was the time I was driving my first car, and someone rear-ended me as I was preparing to make a left turn. I remember hearing a voice telling me to apply the brakes. That kept my car from going into the oncoming traffic. Yes, You were there at that precise moment, and the inner voice I heard was from You.

How about the time I went swimming in the South China Sea, even though I could barely swim? You calmed my fears and helped me to float.

You are my Protector. Your words in Psalm 91 have become my guide. Thank You for being there then—and now.

You are my Comfortor, and there is no one who can comfort as You.

My world fell apart when my parents passed away—Dad in 1993 and Mom in 2001. However, You were there for me as I was grieving, and You comforted me like no other person could. You put my world back together.

You also comforted and protected me during my military service. When I was homesick, Your words strengthened me as I read my Bible in the barracks. In the midst of those lonely nights, I drew strength in knowing You were there. As I performed my duties during the day, I kept in mind Your everpresence.

Even though You are God, I have found no better friend than You.

~Ed Chappelle

God, You were there as Life Giver even when I was too young to remember. When I needed a blood transfusion at birth because my blood was not right and could not support life, You guided my parents to make the best medical decisions. You gave me this first blood transfusion, and I lived.

But what's more important than the physical blood transfusion You gave me, is the fact that You introduced me to Your Son, Jesus Christ. Thank You for the salvation that is found exclusively through Him. Thank You that Your Holy Spirit made His presence tangible to me.

Lord Jesus, You gave Your blood on the cross, and as it spilled onto the ground, You gave me a spiritual blood transfusion. Only Your shed blood was able to provide me with eternal life as You conquered death, hell, and the grave, resurrecting and ascending into heaven to prepare a place for me, and I look forward to the day when You come again and I can see Your face.

My Savior, You have been there in the good times and the sad times, and I thank You for making the ultimate sacrifice for me.

You say in Your Word, "This is my commandment: Love each other in the same way I have loved you. There is no greater love than to lay down one's life for one's friends. You are My friends if you do whatever I command" (John 15:14 NKJV).

My Jesus, You sacrificed Your life, to save me.

Through life's stormy nights of loneliness, as well as through those days of happiness, God, You have shown me unconditional love, and You have demonstrated that You will always be there for me.

God, without reservation, I can say You are my Best Friend. Even though You are God, I have found no better friend than You.

Thank You Father God, Jesus, and Holy Spirit for being my strength and my shield, and for shepherding me through life's challenges, and for the mercy and grace You have instilled in my life.

You have always been and always will be faithful to me, and for that I can declare with surety I am one blessed man.

Write a thank You note to God, addressing Him as "Friend."

Thank You, God, for being present in all circumstances. I give You praise for being the strength of my life.

In Jesus's Name, Amen.

Life is a Juggling Act

Maria T. Henriksen

Splat! I dropped one of the eggs I was "juggling"—at least that's what it felt like I was doing. Now I had to clean up the mess.

You see, not only had I dropped an egg, I had let go of priorities. I was juggling a day job, a family life, and writing a book. Therefore, my house was in disarray. Something had to give.

In recent months, my novel had become my ministry. My biggest desire was to have teenage readers come to know Christ as they read it. What was more important than that?

Perhaps you know the feeling. You are doing too many things for an extended period of time, and it becomes obvious you can't do them all. Something would eventually suffer.

In my case, it was a clean, well-kept home.

Unfortunately, scripture doesn't provide a handbook entitled, *How to Live a Balanced Life*. Those principles are in the Bible, but we have to dig for them in order to find them.

Colossians 3:23-24 NIV provides some insight. "Whatever you do, work at it with all your heart, as working for the Lord, not for human masters, since you know that you will receive an inheritance from the Lord as a reward. It is the Lord Christ you are serving."

Just like the egg on the floor begging to be cleaned up, the things I had neglected haunted me. I viewed them as constant reminders of

99

how I had failed; how I couldn't do it all. I felt bogged down. I was becoming resentful of the mundane tasks—even ministry responsibilities that tore me away from other important matters, such as my family.

Furthermore, as a result of life's demands, I had set aside the most important activitiy. I needed to remember to prioritize my relationship with my Best Friend, Jesus Christ.

I needed to remember to prioritize my relationship with my **Best** *Friend, Jesus Christ.*

~Maria T. Henriksen

My friend, is it this way with you also? Finding time to worship Jesus Christ needs to advance to first place on the to-do list. We need to make this decision.

God gives us these words of hope, "Whatever you do, whether in word or deed, do it all in the name of the Lord Jesus, giving thanks to God the Father through him" (Colossians 3:17 NIV).

When we prioritize Jesus Christ, He shows us how to work effectively, and how to balance our schedule.

Breathe.

Relax.

Take time to recharge your faith. With Him, you can do this.

And now that you've spent quality time with your Best Friend...

Figure out which loose ends need to be tied up. Show those things you once neglected some attention, so they will no longer nag you.

You've got this!

As you prioritize your friendship with Jesus, the puzzle pieces of life become a beautiful array rather than an unrecognizable mess.

Name three ways you can re-center your thoughts on Jesus Christ.

Heavenly Father, Thank You for being available for me. Sometimes I get caught up with my responsibilities that I let go of my time with with You. Give me the discernment to prioritize You so I'll know how to clean up the messiness of life, and become effective in family, homemaking, my job, my ministry, and matters of faith.

In Jesus's Name, Amen.

Don't Bite the Bait

Karen Jurgens

A Word fitly spoken is like apples of gold in settings of silver.

~Proverbs 25:11 NKJV

"So, this is supposed to be my bait?" I sniffed a plastic bowl of shrimp, wrinkled my nose, and coughed.

The jolly man behind the store counter chuckled as he crinkled his eyes and flashed tobacco-stained teeth.

"Yup. The fish love 'em. And I heered they's really a-bitin' today." He winked. "Good luck."

The screen door creaked behind me as I waved 'so long' and headed to find our boat. My fishing partner excelled at this sport, and I was counting on his expertise. I was glad to experience something new with my friend.

Did I mention that I had never been in a fishing boat—nor had fished before? Perhaps I could fake it. Better yet, maybe I'd have beginner's luck and catch one. The thought cheered me.

"Halloo!" A hand waved in the distance.

Next to the pier, Eddie stood in the middle of a wobbling rowboat, legs spread wide for balance. I hurried to catch his hand and hoist myself onto a wooden seat, warmed by the autumn sun.

Off we went, paddling across a placid lake. The sun reflected off its surface like a thousand tiny mirrors.

An inviting spot beckoned us to try our luck. As he baited his hook, I tried to imitate the procedure with my shrimp in one hand and hook in the other.

"Here, let me help," Eddie said. He graciously got me all set and cast my line into the water.

Fishing was a silent sport, so I held my pole, sat back, and quietly admired God's beautiful landscape. Leaves changing from green into gold lined the banks, and birds soared in a sky dolloped with marshmallow clouds. Joy rose in my soul. *Thank you, Lord, for your amazing creation.*

I also prayed to catch just *one* fish.

The warm stillness, the water's lapping, and the gentle rocking hypnotized me. But, as soon as the bobber bounced, and the line tugged, I knew I had a catch. I shot my friend a frantic glance.

"Reel it in...slowly now. That's the way. Good girl!" Instead of taking my pole, he talked me through it.

"Oh my!" I held my real tight as the pole curved downward. "Ugh!"

I yanked hard, and my prize flew out of the water, landing in the bottom of the boat, flopping helplessly. The poor thing wriggled, squirmed, and tried with all its might to jerk free. The hook had sliced all the way through its mouth, like a catch on a string of pearls. Escape was impossible.

"Hey, he's a beauty! Let's take a picture of you beside your catch."

Eddie grabbed his iPhone, and I displayed a victorious smile. For a few short moments, I reveled in my ability to trick a fish with a bait-covered hook.

But as I examined my trophy, my pride deflated. His round eyes widened with the terror of impending death, as if he knew his coffin would be a hot frying pan. How could I be the one responsible for the tragic fate of this innocent fish? I couldn't remove the hook and I became queasy with the effort.

"Please let him go," I pleaded.

Eddie sighed, loosened the metal hook, and tossed him back in the lake.

I swear that little guy would have won gold at the Summer Olympics. Did I imagine that he threw me a look of gratefulness before he zipped away? Hopefully he had learned his lesson for next time: *Don't bite the bait.*

As I sat through the rest of the day pretending to try to catch another fish, the Lord dropped a question into my spirit. *Just as fishermen use bait to snare fish, can the enemy also snare men with deceptive bait?*

A Scripture from Proverbs leaped out of my memory, "You are snared by the words of your mouth; You are taken by the words of your mouth. So do this, my son, and deliver yourself; For you have come into the hand of your friend: Go and humble yourself; Plead with your friend. Give no sleep to your eyes, Nor slumber to your eyelids. Deliver yourself like a gazelle from the hand of the hunter,

And like a bird from the hand of the fowler" (Proverbs 6:2-5 NASB). (My recent experience tempted me to add, *and like a fish from a baited hook.*)

The Lord dropped a question in my spirit. Just as fishermen use bait to snare fish, can the enemy also snare men with deceptive bait?

~Karen Jurgens

Just like a fish, the enemy's delicious-looking bait can deceive us to take a bite, only to find his sharp hook hidden inside. But God can take His forgiving hand of grace and free us from a frying pan of sin. Even though we may become accidentally hooked by a tempting lure and say something we shouldn't—a lie, gossip, or angry words—isn't is reassuring to know that God is our Deliverer?

As we swim through life's ocean speaking a sea of words, may God give us wisdom to avoid biting at deceptive bait. May we be "shrewd as serpents and innocent as doves" (Matthew 10:16 NASB).

Have you been snared by your words? Share how Jesus set you free.

Lord, give me wisdom not to bite the enemy's glittering bait, but let me use my words to bless others and be refreshed in You. May I always use my words to praise, worship, and glorify Your Name.

In Jesus's Name, Amen.

The Burning Coals Project

Julie Souza Bradley Lilly

But I tell you, love your enemies and pray for those who persecute you.

~Matthew 5:44 NIV

It was the hardest year of my life.

It was in 2013 that my husband Jim succumbed to cancer. I would love to tell you that after my husband died, countless people rallied around me, as a new widow, to help me in such a brutally hard time, but they did not. Apart from my parents and a couple of close friends, I was on my own to navigate the choppy waters of grief.

I had always imagined widows being treated kindly. Instead, I was judged for not grieving correctly, and told I was taking too long to grieve, and even falsely accused of things—while utterly ridiculous— that were still painful and insulting.

It's been six years, and even though I am happily remarried, I still have emotional wounds that bleed on occasion from that season in my life.

Recently, I found out that one of my greatest offenders is going through similar grief and loss. Out of the blue, the Lord plunked an offer into my heart—relating to a modification of the Golden Rule. Based on Matthew 7:12,

The Golden Rule, He says, "Do unto others as you would have them do unto you." What God told me is that relative to my grieving offender, there is a secret to my receiving emotional healing. The Lord spoke into my spirit: "Do unto others as you would HAVE HAD them do unto you."

"Do unto others as you would HAVE HAD them do unto you."

-Julie Lilly, paraphrase of Matthew 7:12

Read that again. Part of my healing would come in ministering to the needs of my offender in the way I needed, but did not receive, when I was hurting. It is natural to bristle at the idea. They are reaping what they sowed. They are getting their just desserts.

Then the Lord reminded me I was not left with the just desserts for my sins. Jesus Christ came to spare me from hell and damnation. Even though I have sinned against Him countless times, His love won out over revenge. He bore the penalty on Himself that rightfully belonged to His offender, namely ME.

Christianity is not for wimps. But I have zero question if this offer in my heart was from God or my imagination. Forgiveness and responding to cruelty with love and kindness are part of taking up our cross to follow Him—dying to our flesh in order to honor Him and bless another.

I have already begun. By the time you read this, I will be over ten weeks into my "Burning Coals Project."

"If your enemy is hungry, give him food to eat; if he is thirsty, give him water to drink. In doing this, you will heap burning coals on his head, and the Lord will reward you" (Proverbs 25:21-22 NIV).□□□□□□□□□□□□□ The coals are not heaped upon our enemy to burn them, but to bring a blessing of warmth to their home.

Beloved, if you have been wounded by unsafe people, I am not suggesting that you subject yourself again to harm or abuse. But I am suggesting that from afar, you pray forgiveness and blessing over your offenders' lives.

There is treasure buried here few find. Jesus left it here, in this wounded place, for us to discover. Get out your shovel. Do the hard thing and dig through the heart of stone to find the heart of flesh (see Ezekiel 36:26a). Jesus set this example and was rewarded with the place of greatest honor, at the right hand of the Father. If we follow His example, we will be blessed, too.

How is one way you can show love to an enemy?

Father God, strengthen me to do this wise thing that is so hard and painful. I cannot do it on my own. I need Your help to be able to deny my flesh, take up my cross and follow You, not merely in my words, but in my deeds. Lord, make me into a true follower of Christ. Not my will, but thine be done.

In Jesus's Name, Amen.

A Prayer for the Prodigal

Julie Souza Bradley Lilly

Father God, it's getting cold outside.

I look out the window at the frosty rooftops of my neighbors, and my heart sinks to think of those without a roof over their heads or hope in their hearts. I think of those held prisoner in the clutches of addiction, those without food to eat, and whose only socks are threadbare with holes.

Father, we lift the homeless, the lost, the sick, the addicted and the vulnerable. We lift those who left rashly, wandered away or were taken. We lift those in rebellion, those who were abused or forgotten. Have mercy upon them, Lord! We pray for their safety. We pray for their provision.

Deliver them from evil. Send an angel of mercy. Still the tongue of the deceiver. Convince them of Your love. Lift the fog and break the chains that keep them in darkness. Arise, Spirit of Repentance. Set their hearts and minds toward home.

Good Shepherd, leave the ninety-nine, and go out into the wilderness in search of this one who has gone astray (Matt 18:12). Tune your ear to hear their cries in the darkness. When they are cold and weak, lift them up, dear Shepherd. Wrap them in Your mantle and carry them on Your shoulders.

We pray Matthew 18:11-14 KJV, "For the Son of Man is come to save that which was lost. How think ye? If a man have a hundred sheep, and one of them be gone astray, doth he not leave the ninety and nine, and goeth into the mountains, and seeketh that which is gone astray? And if so be that he find it, verily I say unto you, he rejoiceth more of that *sheep* than of the ninety and nine which went not astray. Even so it is not the will of your Father which is in heaven, that one of these little ones should perish."

Father, for those who grieve for a loved one who is lost, comfort them in Your presence. Refresh their hope to continue to believe in a God of miracles. We ask that they will see their heart's desire fulfilled, and that the empty chair at the table will be filled once again. Give them Your heart, Father, to joyfully embrace the prodigal who returns home.

Father, we lift up ourselves. Within every one of us there remains a bit of prodigal—some bit, as of yet, unyielded flesh that remains outside the warmth of surrender.

~Julie Lilly

And Father, we lift up ourselves. Within every one of us there remains a bit of prodigal—some bit, as of yet, unyielded flesh that remains outside the warmth of surrender. We long to hear Your voice and find Your soothing comfort.

We humble ourselves before You.

Anoint our heads with oil. Shine Your light of revelation upon our dark places. We come, recognizing our need, and we ask for healing and forgiveness. May there remain in us no place for the enemy to gain a foothold, but that every part of us would be safe within the fold.

Share a testimony of a prodigal who returned to faith in Jesus Christ.

Lord, we all like sheep have gone astray. Shepherd, come again and gently lead us home.

In Jesus's Name, Amen.

Picking Up Rocks:

The Blessings of Obedience

Shanda Neighbors

The woman took short steps propelled by the use of a cane. Head down. Gaze fixed on the uneven ground beneath her. It was clear she was searching for something.

Then came the familiar nudge. "Help her."

So many times, this nudge has prompted me to do things that seem a bit odd. I questioned whether this was one of those times. I accommodated the tugging of my heart and risked the awkward question. "Can I help you find something?"

"No. Thank you. I'm just picking up rocks."

This was not the answer I anticipated. No help needed. We were in the mountains. Rocks were everywhere. She explained that she had a habit of finding and polishing interesting rocks. We made small talk as I nursed my silent conclusion. *The nudge has done it again. Nothing to see here.*

This explains why I struggle with obedience to the Lord. I end up doing things that don't seem to matter or even make sense, and I miss out on things that I feel do matter. *My ear for the Spirit must be impaired,* I thought. Insecurity was speaking. Disappointment arose. This would have been a great time to recite Samuel's words to King

Saul, "To obey is better than sacrifice ... rebellion is as the sin of witchcraft" (1 Samuel 15:22-23 KJV).

Perhaps then I would know I was released. I looked for a polite escape back to my life and agenda, but the lady and I soon became engrossed in conversation. We chatted for a while before God unveiled a tiny portion of His plan. The talk was merely a prelude to unveiling her real need and simply made her feel comfortable enough to share it.

She, a fellow writer, was seeking a community of writers for accountability purposes. In fact, she had prayed for it. Amazingly, from hundreds of conference attendees representing many locations, she and I lived near each other. The writers' group I attended was about midway between us. I was able to connect her with our group, and I have been a grateful beneficiary of her regular attendance. Her words are otherworldly. She is rich in wisdom, and her pen oozes encouragement.

When I approached her that day, I thought it was about me helping her. I was wrong. God knew that in the months ahead, I would need her counsel, her support, and her prayers as much as she needed mine. She is a treasure.

This simple encounter was a reminder that our blessings are often tied to our obedience.

~Shanda Neighbors

This simple encounter was a reminder that our blessings are often tied to our obedience. I wonder how many of them I've missed because I failed to obey the Lord. It is so easy to reason away the little things He asks of us. How quickly we forget that there are no little things with an almighty God. He works the miraculous with even the dust of the ground. The smallest things we offer Him can become the great wonders of our lives. John 14:15 ESV encourages us to obey, "If you love me, you will keep my commandments."

It's helpful for us to remember His commandments are for us. They do please God, but they are for our benefit. This is true of everything God asks. No matter how grand, insignificant or difficult the task appears, it will glorify God when we obey the prompting of the Spirit, but it will also bless us.

God is love.

Love will never ask us to do anything that hasn't considered our well-being. When we truly believe this, we heed His voice no matter how odd it appears.

Jesus linked love to obedience. It is the only acceptable human response to divine love. It is also the genuine measure of our heart toward God.

Share an act of your obedience that led to an unexpected blessing.

Father God, give me the courage to do what You've ask me to do—even when it seems trite. Help me to keep Your commandments, and cause me to love You through my obedience.

In Jesus's Name, Amen.

She's More than a Friend

Stephanie Pavlantos

The heartfelt counsel of a friend is as sweet as perfume and incense.

~Proverbs 27:9 NLT

I didn't know I needed a friend like her, but God knew. To me she was like sweet perfume.

I was out of school, single, looking for a job, and trying to get involved in church. I wasn't sure about my relationship with God, even though my parents had reared me in a Christian home. It was confusing being told most of my life to be good, wear the right clothes, act godly, go to church, and watch my language, because none of these outward instructions helped me to have the vital relationship with Jesus that I desired.

Marilyn was the kind of woman who smiled with her eyes, not just with her mouth. Although she was fifteen years older than me and married with children, God sent her into my life to show me who Jesus Christ was and how much He loved me.

Her way of teaching drew me in. As I listened in her Sunday School classes, Bible stories came to life. She renewed my understanding of characters such as Daniel, Isaiah, and others. Her teaching on spiritual warfare showed me I could be victorious in this life through activating Bible promises. I was alert, listening, and learning.

Most of all, Marilyn opened my eyes to understand the Savior wanted a personal relationship with me. I realized His love was not based on my works, but on His. Jesus wanted to be my friend. No one had explained Jesus was interested in me and the intricacies of my life. I discovered He wanted me to talk to Him and spend time resting in His presence. Jesus really loved me!

Marilyn and I laughed, cried, and prayed together often. She was always there for me, and so patient—even when I showed up at her house unexpectedly during the dinner hour.

Although Marilyn and I don't live nearby anymore, she is still my spiritual mom and friend.

Do you have a "Marilyn" in your life who has modeled Jesus's character to you? Value them, my friend, for they are a God-sent treasure.

~Stephanie Pavlantos

Do you have a "Marilyn" in your life who has modeled Jesus's character to you? Value them, my friend, for they are a God-sent treasure.

Today, more than ever before, our world needs men and women who model the character of Jesus. It's what our teens, college kids, and young adults need. Like us, they desire to have someone love them for who they are, to come beside them, and walk out life with them. No judgment, no criticism—just acceptance and love.

This is what Jesus did.

He was sent to walk the dusty streets of Earth so we could touch heaven and learn His heart of love for us. I pray my children will meet someone like Marilyn, who will model Jesus to them as she did for me.

Jesus's desire is for us to do as He did and to make disciples of all the nations. He wants us to be like Marilyn to those in our sphere of influence.

He says in Matthew 28, "Go therefore and make disciples of all nations … teaching them to observe all that I have commanded you" (Matthew 28:18b, 20b ESV).

God may never call us to another country, but making disciples in our families and in our own neighborhoods is the perfect place to start. Are you willing? To those who are listening, we are a sweet savor of Christ's sacrificial love.

Who are you discipling? Be the friend who is as sweet perfume to someone in need.

Heavenly Father, Thank You for giving me the gift of Your Son, Jesus Christ, my Savior and Friend. Thank You for guiding me in prayer. Thank You for friends who have led me to You, who have helped me to grow, and have modeled Jesus's character. Bless them now.

In Jesus's Name, Amen.

He Loves Me

Glenda Shouse

That Christ may dwell in your hearts through faith; that you, being rooted and grounded in love, may be able to comprehend with all the saints what is the width and length and depth and height— to know the love of Christ which passes knowledge; that you may be filled with all the fullness of God.

~Ephesians 3:17b-19 NKJV

He loves me, he loves me not, he loves me, he loves me not...

I remember plucking a daisy and pulling off the petals and saying these words. It's something children enjoy doing. I know I did. Of course, I was trying to see if my imaginary boyfriend loved me. Being a child, I really did not understand love, but I knew my family loved me.

As an adult, it was difficult to realize God loved me even when I messed up. There was something in my heart that held me back from accepting my heavenly Father's unconditional love. I could not understand God loves me all the time. His love is not based on my performance. He continues to love me. Whether I'm good, bad, or indifferent, God loves me still.

During a time of prayer with two of my sisters in the Lord, one of them drew me a picture. It was a daisy with lots of petals. Some of the petals were falling off, and on each petal was written "He loves me." My sister looked at me and said, "There are no 'He loves-me-not's.'"

That beautiful example and those wonderful words changed my life. I will always remember and know without a doubt that He loves me. God does love me! What an amazing and beautiful love He has for us. The Bible says, "For God so loved the world that He gave His only begotten Son" (John 3:16 KJV).

Whether I'm good, bad, or indifferent, God loves me still.

~Glenda Shouse

And you know, friend, Father God does love you.

He loves you so much He sent His only begotten Son, Jesus Christ, to die on the cross to save you. You can receive and know this love by praying from your heart and telling Jesus you need Him to be your Savior. Ask Him to forgive your sins. He will answer your prayer, and He will come into your heart and abide with you as your Lord and Savior. Your life will be changed forever.

Share a remembrance of how God reassured you He loves you unconditionally.

Father God, thank You that Your love for me is eternal, unlimited, unconditional. I rest in the knowledge that You will always love me.

In Jesus's Name, Amen.

The Reward of Friendship

Sandra Stein

Therefore, as God's chosen people, holy and dearly loved, clothe yourselves with compassion, kindness, humility, gentleness and patience.

~Colossians 3:12 NIV

God ordained a friendship I never guessed could have happened.

Occasionally I would visit a pet store where my husband worked. The store owner was nice but his wife, Glen? Let's just say I found her a bit odd. We would speak a few sentences to each other, and she would usually go on her way in mid-conversation.

This couple stopped by our house one day, which was something they had never done before. The two men took a walk, and by default, I kept the missus company.

The situation made me uncomfortable. After a few minutes of small talk, she told me why they had stopped by. Her husband had cancer. It broke my heart as I watched the tears falling down her cheeks. Her husband's cancer was fast-spreading, and within a year, he passed away.

After that, Glen kept asking my husband to bring me with him to the store. At first, I was reluctant because I barely knew her, but I knew she needed female companionship so I went along.

Glen made efforts to talk to me, and I took the opportunity to ask her if she believed in Jesus Christ. When her husband was alive, she had no desire to seek Jesus or any religion. But now, on her own, she wanted to learn more about my Savior. I invited her to church, and she accepted.

Within a few short weeks, we had become friends. This brought to my remembrance, "One who has unreliable friends soon comes to ruin, but there is a friend who sticks closer than a brother" (Proverbs 18:24 NIV).

Glen called me one morning, crying.

She, too, had been diagnosed with cancer. She was scared, and with no one to turn to, I became her caregiver. I knew God wanted me to do this for her. Since Glen didn't drive, I took her to doctor and chemo appointments and picked up her medications.

Within three years, my new-found friend had lost her husband, had surgery, suffered a stroke, lost her business, and then she lost her home. Sick and having nowhere else to go, Social Services got her into a nursing home. She took what few belongings that she could fit in her tiny room and she settled in.

In her last days, Glen was adamant about reading the Bible with me. We spent our afternoons discussing scriptures, talking about eternity, and enjoying fellowship.

After finishing our Bible studies, she always told me, "God has a plan for me." I'd smile, but when I got to my car, I'd cry. I was determined to make her as happy as I could.

We were the typical odd couple, but by God's intervention, He had brought us together—not only to be friends, but to learn from each other.

Caring for Glen showed me the life-lesson of bravery.

Glen had gone from being a successful businesswoman and homeowner to losing everything and owning nothing, yet she continued to learn and grow, and she was happier after these trials than before they came.

During all the trials Glen faced, not once did she complain. Not once did she blame anyone, and especially not God. She found comfort in God's Son, Jesus Christ, the love He had for her, and the fact she would meet Him face-to-face when she went to heaven.

We were the typical odd couple, but by God's intervention, He had brought us together.

~Sandra Stein

Before Glen's homegoing, she saw her brother place his faith in Jesus Christ, and she joyfully witnessed his baptism. He had decided to make a decision for Christ because he had heard us talking about the Lord.

I believe God's plan for Glen's life was to be a brave witness of unswerving faith to her brother so they both would be saved.

Faith and friendships came by hearing the Word of God.

Romans 10:17 NKJV reads, "So then faith comes by hearing, and hearing by the word of God."

Even through trials and hardships I can't explain, God still worked His best by saving two souls. Had it not been for the odd friendship He designed by putting Glen and me together, we would not have seen His work of salvation for Glen or her brother.

What friend has God put in your life that at first felt like an odd match? How have you learned to trust God's leading?

Lord God, You created us for fellowship—to have and to be a friend. Thank You for putting people in my life You want me to befriend. Help me to set aside any judgmental thoughts and accept others for the treasures You created them to be. Help me to share my faith in Jesus Christ, the Bible, and biblical values with every friend You have ordained for me to have in my life.

In Jesus's Name, Amen.

Fallen Heroes

Diane Virginia

In Ronald Reagan's 1986 Memorial Day speech given at Arlington National Cemetery, the President says, "It's the young who do the fighting and dying when a peace fails and a war begins." He lists hero after hero, outlining through these examples why we honor our fallen military men and women.

Reagan shares, "Not far from here is the statue of the three servicemen. … Perhaps you've seen it—three rough boys walking together, looking ahead with a steady gaze…. The three are touching each other, as if they're supporting each other, helping each other on."

Reagan is stirred by this artistic rendition of the three young men because it typifies the commitment and courage of the United States' armed forces, some having given their own lives to save the lives of their loved ones at home.

What does the Bible say about celebrating fallen heroes? We don't have to look far to see it is God's intent to remember our valiant military men and women and to recount their accomplishments.

King David, for example, like Reagan, makes an account of his military men and their achievements. First, he names Adino the Ezinite who spears eight hundred enemies in one battle. He continues his honorarium and names Shammah the Harite who stands his ground in a barley field, refusing to yield it to the Philistines (see 2 Samuel 23:8). David mentions other heroes along

124

with their accomplishments. This is only one biblical example where military heroes are recognized. There are many other places in the Bible where heroes are named and honored.

If God is "The Prince of Peace (Isaiah 9:6b KJV)", then why do we fight wars in the first place? President Regan answers this question towards the end of his speech by saying, "If we really care about peace, we must, through our strength, demonstrate our unwillingness to accept an ending of the peace. We must be strong enough to create peace where it does not exist and strong enough to protect it where it does."

Sometimes peace needs to be enforced, and that by military prowess. When godless men oppress our children, women, and elderly, it is then that we must call upon the courageous amongst us, including our brave young men and women, to save us from these intruders.

Our peace is not free. It is the gift of selfless heroes who look beyond their needs to secure ours.

~Diane Virginia

Our peace is not free. It is the gift of selfless heroes who look beyond their needs to secure ours.

Jesus says, "'The thief does not come except to steal, and to kill, and to destroy; I [Jesus] have come that they may have life and that they may have it more abundantly'" (John 10:10b NKJV).

Our military robs the enemy of his assignment to destroy and secures life for us. It is therefore fitting for us to honor our fallen American mighty men and women, for they, possessing love like our Lord's, have paid the ultimate price to secure our freedom.

When Jesus faced death on Calvary's cross to save humanity, He said, "'Greater love has no one than this, than to lay down one's life for his friends'"(John 15:13 NKJV).

Jesus leads the spiritual army and conquers the ultimate battle—and in the process, secures for us eternal life. Our military men have followed His example.

It is worthy of a national pause to thank God for the United States' armed forces, who have followed in the footsteps of Commander Jesus by giving their lives to save ours.

Share ways you can celebrate friends in the military, for these heros are willing to lay down their lives to protect our liberties.

Thank You, Father God, for our fallen heroes, for these men and women have made the ultimate sacrifice in order to keep America free. Thank You also for those who served, or who are currently serving. These heroes are worth celebrating.

In Jesus's Name, Amen.

Hot Dogs 'n
Holy Spirit Nudges

Diane Virginia

Recently, while I was eating at a local burger restaurant, I felt an inner nudge to visit a clothing store after I finished eating. I did so.

As I arrived, I recognized a homeless man named Mike.

I got wedged between two car mirrors. That caught Mike's attention and he started laughing. We struck up a conversation as I tried to recover my wounded pride. Soon, he asked for money.

"I can't give you money, Mike, but I'll be glad to buy you a meal. Do you like hamburgers?" I pointed toward the restaurant.

"Can I get a hot dog? Or two?"

"Sure. Let's go get you two hot dogs. And we'll get you fries, a drink, and ice cream."

"I don't want no ice cream. It's too cold fer that."

"I understand," I said, but then I wondered if I really understood the bone-chilling cold this gentle soul faced every winter.

We started walking.

As I stepped inside the burger joint, Mike hovered at the door.

"It's okay. Please... come inside."

"I's gonna wait here. I's gonna eat outside."

As is often the case with a homeless person, they are so used to being shamed they are hesitant to enter a building.

"Hey, it's okay. I'm with you. I won't leave, I promise."

Mike entered and cautiously looked around. I wondered if he was looking to see if the management would kick him out.

The server looked at me, puzzled. "Back so soon? Did you decide to get ice cream?"

"My friend is hungry. Mike, tell the lady what you want."

"I wants a hot dog."

"Make that two please...."

Mike was modest with his order. To drink, he asked for a cup of water without ice. He did not order fries because he said he had chips in his backpack that were "not too old to eat." The entire order cost less than five dollars.

While we were waiting for the food order, Mike talked. He shared about his former employment as a painter. But that had been fifteen years prior. He had been unable to get disability even though he had applied several times.

"Perhaps you haven't been able to get disability because you can do something," I said.

"That's what they says, too."

"And?"

"I can't climb ladders no more."

"What's stopping you from trying something new?"

"I drinks."

"I care about you, Mike, so tell it to me straight. Do you want help to overcome that?"

By this time, Mike's hot dogs had arrived. He could have fled, but instead, he bowed his head like he was determining whether I was a safe sounding board. Mike rested his open hands on the bar top. I gently touched his wrist. He grasped my hand with a sincerity that melted my heart and bore his soul.

"All's I got is my drinking."

"I can help you...."

"Ye don't get it do ya?"

"I guess not. Please, help me to understand."

"Some days, it's lonely, an' a good drink takes the edge off. Lotsa days, it's cold 'specially when the winds a knockin' at yer collar like it was last night. If I takes to the bottle, I don't feel it as bad. So, no, I don't wanna give up my booze. We's friends, that bottle an' I. We's old friends."

"Would you believe me if I said you can have a new beginning?"

"Is ye talkin' bout Him?" Mike pointed upwards.

"Yes, I am."

"I likes Him, see?" Mike rolled up his sleeve and revealed a cross tattoo.

Therefore, if anyone is in Christ, he is a new creation; old things have passed away; behold, all things have become new."

~2 Corinthians 5:17

"Jesus has a good plan for you, Mike. And He is just the man who can help you get unstuck. When was the last time you visited Him at church?"

"I walks past a church from where I sleeps in the woods. I wants to go inside. Matter-o-fact, I thinks 'bout that a lot! Purty much always..." Mike's speech trailed off. He was deep in thought.

"And?"

"Theys not gonna want the likes of me." Mike glanced at his attire and frowned.

There it was again, rearing its ugly head—a creature named "Shame" had browbeaten this gentle man once too often.

I could sense Mike's quandary. He could go to the house of God, but he'd be in threadbare clothes while he watched the church members show up in their Sunday best.

He knew he'd be the oddball.

I was ready to act. I knew the same Spirit who had nudged me to drop by the store where Mike was sitting had also been nudging him to attend a certain church. My guess was that there was a preacher being prompted to deliver a sermon that would be exactly what Mike needed to hear. I felt certain some of the congregants would also be sensing the urge to welcome this gentle man into their fold.

God was converging forces in an attempt to rescue a soul who had wandered for fifteen years.

"Mike, listen to me, okay? You go to that church and you hold your head high. God loves you as much as He loves the preacher in the pulpit, and the people who attend. You are welcome there. They are most likely waiting for you to visit. So, this Sunday, go up those church steps and go inside. Even if you've been drinking, go anyway. When you get inside, listen to the message, because I'm sure the pastor has written it just for you."

God was converging forces in an attempt to rescue a soul who had wandered for fifteen years.

~Diane Virginia

"Is ye sure?"

"Yes sir. I am positive. Do you believe me?"

"I hopes so...."

"Hold onto that hope, okay? God is arrainging circumstances just for you. Because He loves you, Mike."

I knew Mike would answer my next question as candidly as he had answered the others.

"Will you go to that church service this Sunday?"

Mike put his hand to his chin. He rubbed it for what seemed like an eternity to me, although in reality, it was only a minute or two.

"Yes. Immna go..."

"Can I pray with you? Because your new beginning will start when you walk through the church doors."

And you will seek Me, and find Me, when you search for Me with all your heart. I will be found of you, says the LORD, and I will bring you back from your captivity."

~Jeremiah 29:13a NKJV

Mike removed his cap and grasped my hands before I asked him to. I felt the cold of his skin and the slenderness of his fingers clinging to my hands, as if holding mine tightly would make his world straighten.

I knew Mike's new beginning would start as soon as he chose to hold as tightly to his Savior's nail-scarred hands.

I prayed for Mike's needs and thanked God that he had permitted me to share part of his day. I prayed for his new beginnings, and for God to wrap His love around my friend.

When Mike departed and I returned to my car, I thanked God for His Holy Spirit nudge.

I hoped that because Mike relied on the generosity of others to provide his meals, this would afford him numerous opportunities to hear about how deep and wide the love of God truly is.

Who is God nudging you to encourage? Will you do it?

Father God, help me to hear and respond to Your inner voice. Fill me with love for those You send my way. Help me to help those who have lost their way, by sharing the good plan You have for them. Help me to not be too busy to respond to Your Holy Spirit-nudges, and to accept Your heavenly assignments.

In Jesus's Name, Amen.

God's Gift of Friendship

Evelyn Wells

A friend loves at all times...

~Proverbs 17:17a NASB

"Do you mind if we pray?" Barbra asked.

I did not know Barbara before that day, but I had been given her phone number and was told she was looking for a carpool partner.

We decided to meet for lunch. That way we could get acquainted. As we sat, Barbara asked if we could pray first. She told me she and her family were Christians, and they were accustomed to praying before meals.

I had asked God for a Christian to carpool with who would be a positive influence in my life and become a friend. Barbara's question was confirmation that He had answered my prayer. I needed someone to share, and to laugh with.

In Job, the prophet writes, "He will yet fill your mouth with laughter and your lips with shouts of joy" (Job 8:21 NIV).

And laugh we did! We shared our stories and refreshed our souls.

Our friendship began even before that first lunch was over. Barbara and I became close friends. She loved everyone and had a wonderful—and sometimes mischievous—smile. She was filled with the love of the Lord and accepted me just as I was—and loved me, anyway—which could not have been easy to do at that time, because I was going through a divorce after an unstable marriage, and my self-esteem was at an all-time low. However, God not only

134

sent me a Christian carpooler; He also sent a forever friend. There was healing in her prayers for me.

As the years went by, our friendship grew. We were no longer carpooling together, and we did not get to see each other as often as we once had, but whenever we did get together, it seemed we picked the conversation right up where we had left off, even if it was a chance meeting or phone conversation.

The years of Barbara's friendship were a blessing, and I miss her. I look forward to seeing her in eternity.

God sent Barbara and many other people into my life because He knew I needed friends like them. And perhaps He knew they needed a friend like me.

~Evelyn Wells

God sent Barbara and many other people into my life because He knew I needed friends like them. And perhaps He knew they needed a friend like me.

I pray I have been, and continue to be, a blessing to many. I am thankful for these friends that God has given me at just the right time in my life. But there is another friend I am most grateful for, whose Name is Jesus Christ.

John writes, "No longer do I call you not servants; for the servant does not know what his master is doing: but I have called you friends; for all things that I have heard from my Father I have made known to you" (John 15:15 NKJV).

God gave us the best friend I could ever imagine when He sent Jesus Christ, His only Son, to live as a man. Jesus lived a perfect life here on Earth so He could redeem us. His perfect, sinless life qualified Him to be able to go to the cross and die a criminal's death on our behalf, taking our sins upon Himself, and then rise again, victorious over death, hell, and the grave.

Friend, if you have not accepted Jesus Christ as your Lord and Savior yet, please pray this prayer with me so I can meet you in eternity, if not sooner, as we travel this life together.

Say from your heart these words:

Lord Jesus Christ,

I ask You to forgive me of my sins. I accept the gift of salvation You purchased for me by shedding Your blood on Calvary's cross and for dying in my place, as the full payment for my sins. Thank You for raising to life and for preparing a place in heaven for me. I look forward to Your soon return. I receive You as my Savior, Lord, and Best Friend. Thank You for loving me.

Amen.

If you prayed this salvation prayer, please let the VineWords Team know. We are delighted you have joined the family of God. Find a good church, so you can grow in your newfound relationship with the best friend ever, Jesus Christ.

Jesus Christ is not only the Savior of those who have accepted God's gift of salvation, He is the Lord of our lives. And, on top of that, He calls us His friends. It cannot get any better than that!

Think of ways to be a friend to those who need to be loved. What action steps can you take to demonstrate your friendship?

Father God, I'm grateful for the love You exhibited by allowing Your only Son, Jesus Christ, to die for my sins so I can live eternally in Your Kingdom. Thank You!

In Jesus's Name, Amen.

Food and Friends

Martin Wiles

Give us each day our daily bread.

~Luke 11:3 NIV

She sliced the cake...and strangers became friends.

I don't mean to brag on my wife's cooking—well, actually, I do—but she is a marvelous cook. One of her specialties is peanut butter cake, and my mom wanted one for her birthday, which we planned to celebrate at a well-liked local restaurant.

My wife called ahead and made reservations. Eleven of us gathered at the tables they pushed together for our group and enjoyed a meal. Mom was excited to be with children, grandchildren, and great-grandchildren.

When everyone finished eating, my wife popped the latches on the Tupperware cake holder and lifted the lid. Comments erupted, but not from our table. I heard them from the threesome sitting at the table beside me. "Ooh look at that cake. Aww, that looks good."

After my wife had sliced and handed everyone at our table a piece of cake, I turned to my neighbors and asked, "Want a piece of cake?" Without thinking, they responded, "Yes, we do."

My act led to conversation. They wanted to know whose birthday it was and how old Mom was. And when they left, they thanked us again for the cake and our kindness. We had made new friends.

Jesus often used eating as an opportunity to make new friends, chat with existing friends, and share His teachings. He even ate with enemies, such as were most of the Pharisees, and by doing so, some of them became His friends. Jesus used this particular occasion to not only enjoy a good meal but also to caution Simon about selfishness.

Luke 7:36 NLT reads, "One of the Pharisees asked Jesus to have dinner with him, so Jesus went to his home and sat down to eat."

Meals with others—friends or potential friends—open doors for conversations of all types. Conversations we might not have time to have or feel comfortable having within the walls of a church building. People are generally more relaxed away from such a formal setting.

Eating together breaks down barriers. After all, how often do we eat with enemies? If we do, the chances are great they might become friends.

Eating together breaks down barriers. After all, how often do we eat with enemies? If we do, the chances are great they might become friends.

~Martin Wiles

A meal together also gives opportunity to show kindness, especially a meal at our home. My wife is the social butterfly in our family and having friends over for a meal is common at our house.

If you want to be like Jesus, prepare some food and ask a few folks over. You never know where your act of kindness and the resulting conversation might lead.

Share a memory where friendships were strengthened over a meal.

Heavenly Father, help me to be generous, especially through sharing meals with friends. Thank You for the Word, which serves as daily bread to my spirit. Thank You also for the Communion meal instituted by Your Son that unites believers as the body of Christ.

In Jesus's Name, Amen.

Meet Our Contributors

Ed · Amanda

Maria · Karen

Julie

Lee Ann · Shanda

Stephanie · Glenda

Sandra

Evelyn

Martin · Diane

Ed Chappelle

Ed Chappelle is the founder/administrator/lead writer of **Come to the Table** Facebook ministry, a place where people of faith are encouraged to connect with others and share testimonies, articles, and prayer needs.

He is an ordained minister, holding credentials since 2010.

Ed is a devotion writer for **VineWords: Devotions and More**. He is a contributing author to *Love Knots: Stories of Faith, Family, and Friendships* (VineWords Publishing).

Some people say Ed's genealogy can be traced to Noah. He and his wife Kym are known for their animal rescue ministry, **Critter Care**. Their "family" includes dogs, cats, birds, a guinea pig, sugar sliders, ferrets, geckos, bearded dragons, tropical fish, and a plethora of God's creatures.

Ed served in the United States Air Force for over four years, earning the rank of Sergeant. He was eight years old when Apollo 11 went to the moon. His love for his country, the armed forces, and space exploration compelled him to write the tribute, *Man on the Moon*.

Amanda Eldridge

Amanda Eldridge is a devotion writer for VineWords: Devotions and More, specializing in topics related to single parenting, homeschooling, and special needs children.

She is a contributing author to *Love Knots: Stories of Faith, Family, and Friendships* (VineWords Publishing).

Amanda is working on a historical fiction novel, set in the North Carolina mountains. She is also writing a romance novel based on her parents' relationship.

Amanda spends her days exploring the world through the eyes of her two elementary-aged home-schooled children, and two special-needs adults whom she cares for. She is a single mom who loves to hike, read novels, and study her Bible.

She is passionate about exploring the foothills, mountains, and coasts of North Carolina, and her children eagerly join her in this quest.

Maria T. Henriksen

Maria T. Henriksen is the author of *Not Again*, a young adult Christian romance novel. She is working on the sequel entitled, *Not Again: The Fallout,* to be published in 2021.

She is a devotion writer for **VineWords: Devotions and More** and a contributing author to *Love Knots: Stories of Faith, Family, and Friendships* (VineWords Publishing).

Maria hosts a ministry through her blog, **Maria's Ministry.** She manages a Facebook group, **Maria's Muses: Inspirational, Christian, & Close to the Heart Readers**, which consists of Christian writers and contributors.

Maria graduated from Shippensburg University with a bachelor's in Communications/Journalism with a concentration in Public Relations and a minor in Psychology.

Maria has experience in graphic arts, finance, banking, health, fitness, beauty, and substitute teaching.

As a wife for over two decades, Maria considers herself blessed. She and her husband are the proud parents of twin boy/girl teenagers. In her spare time, she runs, writes poems and songs, creates graphics, enjoys family activities, and reads. Maria's greatest desire is for lives to be transformed through her inspirational writings.

Karen Jurgens

Karen Jurgens, a Cincinnati native, is a Texan transplant for thirty-five years and counting. Retired from a teaching career, she is a Christian writer, editor, and speaker. Passionate about how to find God's peace through life's storms, she blogs at **Touched by Him**, *her ministry blog.*

Karen is a senior editor, Bible study and devotion writer for **VineWords: Devotions and More**. She is a co-editor, co-compiler, and contributing author for *Love Knots: Stories of Faith, Family, and Friendships* (VineWords Publishing).

Karen holds a B.S. and M.Ed. in Secondary Education with majors in English and French. She is a member of American Christian Fiction Writers (ACFW) and Advanced Writers and Speakers Association (AWSA).

Her first novella, published in an anthology, became the springboard for *Desire's Promise* and *A Perfect Fit*. Blogging led her to **Inspired Prompts Blog**, then **Heart "wings" Ministry** where she served as leader for the "Front Porch" Bible Study Series. She is a contributing author to *Heart"wings" Devotional*. She contributes to other ministries and blogs. Currently, she is revising her *Fruit of the Spirit Bible Study* for publication. Her work-in-progress is a memoir about her "Judas Experience," a celebration of God's supernatural deliverances from the enemy's kiss of deception.

Karen loves to cook, entertain, and enjoy life with her adult daughters and her amazing 98-year-old mother.

Julie Souza Bradley Lilly

Julie Souza Bradley Lilly is the writer of **Prayers of a Ragamuffin Warrior**, a self-professed chief-cook-and-bottle-washer at **Gift of Thorns** Facebook ministry. She is a devotion writer for **VineWords: Devotions and More**, specializing in the area of prayer and a contributing author for *Love Knots: Stories of Faith, Family, and Friendships* (VineWords Publishing).

When asked about who she is, Julie is quick to tell you that she is a worshipper, a servant, blessed wife, step-mom of four adult children, caregiver, retired chiropractor, writer, and most-importantly, a forgiven daughter of God. With thirty-plus years in healthcare, Julie is passionate about seeing the broken come to receive healing and find wholeness in right-relationship with the Creator. Through her own multiple injuries and PTSD, a traumatic brain injury and other health concerns, she has found the generosity of God to be true to His Word in turning all things together for the good for those who love Him and are called according to His purpose.

For those entrusted with a thorn in the flesh, one of Julie's greatest joys is to see the discovery of the treasure the Father hides, tucked in among the thorns. Julie shares that God is good and His mercies endure forever. It is Julie's prayer that the body of believers will honor the Lord and encourage one another toward wholeness, spiritual growth, and mountain-moving faith. For more encouragement, visit Julie's websites. At **Prayers of a Ragamuffin Warrior**, Julie shares encouraging articles with prayers. At **Gift of Thorns**, Julie and her contributor team share powerful and life-changing input, inspiring readers to passionately pursue God.

Lee Ann Mancini

Lee Ann Mancini received a BA in Biblical and Theological Studies from Regent University, a Master's degree in Theological Studies from Trinity Evangelical Divinity School (Trinity International University) in addition to two Master's degrees from Knox Theological Seminary in Biblical and Theological Studies, as well as Christian and Classical Studies.

She is an award-winning Christian children's author. She is the author of the *Sea Kids* book series and the executive producer of the *Sea Kids* animation series, which can be found on Right Now Media, Pure Flix, Trinity Broadcasting Network, and **SeaKidsTV.com**. She also hosts a podcast, **Raising Godly Kids**.

Lee Ann is a devotion writer for **VineWords: Devotions and More**, and a contributing author to *Love Knots: Stories of Faith, Family, and Friendships* (VineWords Publishing).

She holds a board position with South Florida Bible College & Theological Seminary and is an adjunct professor. She also holds a board position with the Alexandrian Forum under the tutelage of Dr. Warren Gage Th.M., J.D., Ph.D. This forum seeks to bring a greater understanding of the Bible by hosting annual Typology Conferences in South Florida, dedicated to the theme of Christ as the center of scripture. Lee Ann speaks to women's groups regarding the redemptive power of the gospel represented through the types of brides of the Church. She maintains memberships with the Christian Women in Media Association and the Advanced Writers and Speakers Association.

Shanda Neighbors

Shanda Neighbors's island upbringing has afforded her the ability to pardon Eve. She too enjoys gardening and picking produce. Her husband eats all she offers him. No questions. She enjoys serving large crowds, but she's a natural overfeeder. She will supply too much nourishment no matter the crowd size. Food is her love-language. She was born and raised in the Bahamas. This has determined both her internal clock and thermostat. She struggles with being on time and is not trusted to set the temperature anywhere. You can always find her outdoors...over 60s and sunny...probably in a jacket. Anyone who invites her to go skiing hates her. Period.

Shanda is a miraculous work in progress. She credits her family with helping that work along. Chief among them is her husband who has demonstrated the power of love and patience. Outside of Jesus, she has had no greater advocate than her beef-and-potatoes husband. Shanda has two daughters who are her treasures.

She is passionate about truth and the reputation of God. This translates into her speaking and writing. Her goal is to live amazed by the love, glory, power, and goodness of our God and of the Lord Jesus Christ, and to share His story with as many people as possible. Shanda is a devotion writer for **VineWords: Devotions and More**, and a contributing author to *Love Knots: Stories of Faith, Family, and Friendships* (VineWords Publishing). She is a devotion speaker at Word Weavers Piedmont-Triad, NC, and she is available for speaking engagements. Her long-term goal is to enter the media industry.

Stephanie Pavlantos

Stephanie Pavlantos is an award-winning author who is passionate about getting people into God's Word. She has taught Bible studies for over fifteen years and speaks at ladies' retreats, her church, and over the internet.

She is an ordained minister, holding credentials since 2019. She is the president of the Hudson, Ohio chapter of Word Weavers.

Stephanie is the social media director/senior editor, Bible study, and devotion writer for **VineWords: Devotions and More**. She is the co-compiler and contributing author to *Love Knots: Stories of Faith, Family, and Friendships* (VineWords Publishing). Her book, *Jewels of Hebrews* (Mount Zion Ridge Press), won third place at Blue Ridge Mountain Christian Writers Conference and an Honorable Mention at the Florida Christian Writers Conference. Stephanie works for the Besorah Institute for Judeo-Christian Studies in the Student Services Department, as well as teaching their online classes. She holds weekly Zoom Bible studies, covering topics such as the Jewish roots of Christianity, the Four Covenants, and other themes. She is published in **Refresh Bible Study Magazine**, **Charisma Magazine**, **Christian Broadcasting Network**, and **Faith Beyond Fear**. Stephanie is a contributing author to **Feed Your Soul with the Word of God** (Lighthouse Bible Studies).

Married for twenty-seven years, she and her husband Mike have three children: Matthew, Alexandria, and Michael. Stephanie has adopted animals of all kinds, including ducks, goats, and chickens.

Glenda Shouse

Glenda Shouse is a devotion writer who is published at **Answers2Prayer, Christian Devotions Ministries, PresbyCan, The Upper Room,** and other ministries.

She is a devotion writer for **VineWords: Devotions and More**. She is a contributing author to *Love-Knots: Stories of Faith, Family, and Friendships* (VineWords Publishing).

Glenda's prayer shawl ministry, **Three-Strand Cord**, focuses on imparting hope to ladies going through difficult times. Each recipient is gifted with a hand-crocheted or knitted prayer shawl she has prayed over with each stitch. When possible, Glenda delivers these shawls personally and prays with the recipients.

Those who know Glenda well are aware of her gifting as a prayer warrior. She is a powerhouse of prayer because of her close relationship with the Lord Jesus Christ.

In her spare time, Glenda enjoys her role as "Grammy" to her two grandsons. She also enjoys reading, crocheting, and knitting.

Sandra Stein

Sandra Stein is a contributing author to the devotionals, *Take My Heart O God* and *Heaven Calling* (Zondervan).

Sandra is a devotion writer for **VineWords: Devotions and More,** and a contributing author to *Love Knots: Stories of Faith, Family, and Friendships* (VineWords Publishing).

She is published at **Vista Magazine** (Wesleyan Publishing) and **Victory in Grace Magazine.**

Sandra's work-in-progress is a victim-to-victory true story entitled, *Emotionally Uphill.* Having been subject to abuse both inside and outside of her home, Sandra felt she had no safe place—that is, until she met Jesus Christ, the Lover of her soul. This book intends to help the reader overcome trauma as Sandra did, by clinging to the One who loves with an everlasting and divine love—Jesus Christ.

With her experience as a dog trainer and with horses, she has a vision for combining her love of animals with her passion to help people.

Sandra's heart's desire is to open a ranch to people who have been bullied or abused, to provide them a place to belong. She envisions emotional and spiritual healings happening through the gentle interaction animals can provide.

Evelyn Mason Wells

Evelyn Mason Wells is an award-winning author who has contributed to *Heart Renovation: A Construction Guide to Godly Character* (2019 Selah finalist, Lighthouse Bible Studies), *Glimmers of Heavenly Light* (Faith Books & More), *Let the Earth Rejoice* (Worthy Inspired), *Breaking the Chains* (2018 Selah finalist, Lighthouse Bible Studies), *Just Breathe* (Worthy/Ellie Claire), and *Feed Your Soul with the Word of God* (Lighthouse Bible Studies).

Evelyn is a Bible study and devotion writer for **VineWords: Devotions and More**. She is a contributing author to *Love Knots: Stories of Faith, Family, and Friendships* (VineWords Publishing).

Evelyn is published at **Refresh Bible Study Magazine** and **Christian Broadcasting Network**.

Passionate about glorifying God through her writing and speaking, Evelyn enjoys spending time on short-term mission trips, both domestic and foreign.

Evelyn loves attending Bible Studies, spiritual retreats, and having good conversation with friends over lunch or a glass of tea. She is an avid fan of the Georgia Bulldogs and Atlanta Braves. She enjoys good books, her cats, traveling, and spending time with her family—especially her grandchildren.

Martin Wiles

Martin Wiles is an author, English teacher, and freelance editor who resides in Greenwood, South Carolina.

He is the founder and editor of the internationally recognized devotion site, **Love Lines from God.**

Wiles is the managing editor for **Christian Devotions**, the senior editor for **Inspire a Fire**, and a proof editor for **Courier Publishing**. He has also served as web content editor for **Lighthouse Publishing of the Carolinas.**

Wiles has authored *A Whisper in the Wood: Quiet Escapes in a Noisy World* (Ambassador International), *Grits & Grace & God,* and *Grits, Gumbo, and Going to Church* (Lighthouse Publishing of the Carolinas), *Morning By Morning, Morning Serenity,* and *Grace Greater Than Sin* (America Star Books), and is a contributing author in *Penned from the Heart* (Son-Rise Publications), *Rise* (Chaplain Publishing), and *Love Knots: Stories of Faith, Family, and Friendships* (VineWords Publishing).

He has served as regional correspondent and Sunday school lesson writer for the **Baptist Courier** and has also written for **Lifeway's Bible Studies for Life** curriculum.

Wiles has been published in **Christian Living in the Mature Years, Mature Living, Open Windows, Proclaim, The Secret Place, The Word in Season, Upper Room, Light from the Word, Reach Out Columbia, Mustard Seed Ministries, Journey Christian Newspaper, Common Ground Herald, The Quiet Hour, Power for Living, Halo Magazine, Joyful Living Magazine, Christian Broadcasting Network, Sharing, Today's Christian Living, These Days, Plum Tree Tavern, Eskimo Pie,**

The Scarlet Leaf Review, Creation Illustrated, LIVE, Purpose Magazine, Stand Firm, The Banner, Relevant, and Lutheran Digest.

He is a regular contributor to **Christian Devotions, PCC Daily Devotions, Theology Mix, Inspire a Fire, The Write Conversation,** and **Vine Words: Devotions and More,** and is a regular writer for the **Dorchester County Eagle Record,** the **Orangeburg County Times** and **Democrat,** and the **Greenwood County Index Journal.**

Wiles's latest book, ***Don't Just Live...Really Live*** is under contract with Ambassador International.

Diane Virginia

Diane Virginia (Cunio) is an award-winning author and the founder/ administrator/ lead senior editor of **VineWords: Devotions and More.**

She is an ordained minister, holding credentials since 2005.

Diane is a co-editor, co-compiler, and contributing author to *Love-Knots: Stories of Faith, Family, and Friendships*.

Diane's book, *The Kiss of Peace: A Contemporary Exploration into Song of Solomon,* won The Sparrow Award, Second Runner Up, at the Asheville Christian Writer's Conference 2019. The sequel, *Behind the Veil: Becoming the Ascended Bride of Song of Solomon*, is in the works.

She has developed the model for motion-activated musical prayer centers for use in the garden retreat, themed to the places where the Bride of Christ travels in the allegory, Song of Solomon. She envisions these prayer gardens as a refuge for seekers and believers alike to find or deepen their relationship with Jesus Christ.

Diane is published at **Answers2Prayer, Christian Broadcasting Network, Christian Devotions Ministries, Faith Beyond Fear, Pentecostal Publishing House, PresbyCan Daily Devotional, The Secret Place, VineWords: Devotions and More,** and other ministries.

Friend, if you've enjoyed reading *Love Knots*, please consider leaving an Amazon review. We appreciate you and pray God's blessings to be upon you daily.